EASY CHRISTMAS CRAFTS for the FAMILY

*T*his holiday season, craft your way to a merry Christmas with quick and easy handmade treasures from the experts at Leisure Arts. Oh, what fun you'll have impressing people on your gift list and visitors to your delightfully decorated home. More than 125 of our best creations sparkle with professional quality, yet glow with the warmth and charm that come from being handmade. Completing the projects couldn't be easier, thanks to our simple-to-follow instructions, comprehensive materials lists, and beautiful full-color photographs. Plus, we've included three special sections featuring crafts that can be completed in an hour or less — so you'll have plenty of time to enjoy the pleasures of this captivating season. Simply begin turning the pages now to get your holidays off to a crafty start!

LEISURE ARTS, INC.
Little Rock, Arkansas

EASY CHRISTMAS CRAFTS for the FAMILY

EDITORIAL TEAM

Editorial Director: Susan Frantz Wiles
Associate Editor: Kimberly L. Ross

ART TEAM

Art Publications Director: Rhonda Shelby
Art Imaging Director: Mark Hawkins
Art Category Manager: Lora Puls
Freelance Artist: Jessica Riddle
Art Imaging Technicians: Stephanie Johnson and Mark Potter
Publishing Systems Administrator: Becky Riddle
Publishing Systems Assistants: Clint Hanson, John Rose, and
    Chris Wertenberger

BUSINESS STAFF

Publisher: Rick Barton
Vice President, Finance: Tom Siebenmorgen
Director of Corporate Planning and Development:
    Laticia Mull Dittrich
Vice President, Retail Marketing: Bob Humphrey
Vice President, Sales: Ray Shelgosh
Vice President, National Accounts: Pam Stebbins
Director of Sales and Services: Margaret Reinold
Vice President, Operations: Jim Dittrich
Comptroller, Operations: Rob Thieme
Retail Customer Service Managers: Sharon Hall and Stan Raynor
Director of Public Relations and Retail Marketing: Stephen Wilson
Print Production Manager: Fred F. Pruss

International Standard Book Number: 1-57486-367-3

10 9 8 7 6 5 4 3 2 1

Table of Contents

Table of Contents

51

TRIM THE TREE 56

Table of Contents

Table of Contents

Table of Contents

128

Deck
THE HALLS

Come along with us and see how easy it is to dress every room in your house in festive style. You'll love the unique card "clothesline," and we've given lots of ideas for traditional stockings and wreaths. You can whip up colorful pillows for any spot, step into the den to skirt the tree, or "get cooking" in the kitchen with decorative accents. And if you're ready for more, you can carry Christmas cheer into the garden with painted stepping stones. Before you know it, you'll have merry touches all through the house!

Natural Appeal

*P*inecones, dried flowers, and *jute twine lend rustic appeal to our evergreen wreath. Homestyle touches include padded paper-bag gingerbread men and fabric-wrapped foam balls. It's a real country charmer!*

WHAT TO BUY

24" dia. artificial evergreen wreath, six 2" dia. plastic foam balls, ¼ yd. of cotton batting, and dried German statice

THINGS YOU HAVE AT HOME

Scraps of assorted fabrics, straight pins, tracing paper, brown paper bags, pinking shears, craft glue, paper-backed fusible web, buttons, black permanent fine-point pen, pinecones, jute twine, and a hot glue gun

RUSTIC HOLIDAY WREATH

1. For each ball ornament, tear six 1" x 9" strips of fabric. Overlapping long edges and twisting fabric at bottom of foam ball, wrap strips around ball; secure with straight pins.

2. Trace pattern, page 168, onto tracing paper; cut out. For each gingerbread man ornament, draw around pattern twice on brown paper and once on batting. Cut out batting shape. Use pinking shears to cut out paper shapes slightly inside drawn line. Positioning batting shape between paper shapes, use craft glue to glue layers together.

3. Referring to *Fusing Basics,* page 187, use patterns, page 168, to make one heart and two cheek appliqués for each gingerbread man ornament from fabric scraps. Position cheeks and heart on each gingerbread man; fuse in place. Glue three buttons onto each gingerbread man; use pen to draw "stitches," eyes, and mouths.

4. Arrange ornaments, pinecones, and sprigs of statice on wreath; glue in place.

5. Following *Making Multi-Loop Bows,* page 191, tie a 68" length of jute into a bow with six 8" loops and two 20" streamers. Position bow and streamers on wreath; glue in place.

WELCOMING COMMITTEE

*E*ven if you won't have a white Christmas, you can share some snowy fun with visitors when you add this friendly character to your welcoming committee. Our easy-to-finish snowman is crafted from an ordinary fence picket and "dressed" with a stocking cap and a fringed fabric scarf.

WHAT TO BUY

6-ft. fence picket, white spray paint, artificial textured snow, 1/4 yd. of fabric, stocking cap, plastic foam carrot, and a small artificial poinsettia

THINGS YOU HAVE AT HOME

Handsaw, sandpaper, paintbrush, utility knife, fourteen assorted black buttons, two small branches, and a hot glue gun

SNOWMAN PICKET

Allow paint to dry after each application.

1. Use handsaw to cut 1 ft. from fence picket. Sand board smooth.

2. Spray picket with one or two coats of paint. Use paintbrush to apply artificial snow to one side (front) of picket; allow to dry.

3. Tear a 1"w strip from long edge of fabric; cut strip into eight 5" long pieces. Use one piece to tie a knot around center of remaining pieces; glue to top of cap. Glue poinsettia to cuff of cap. Place cap on one end of picket.

4. Use knife to cut off large end of carrot, leaving flat surface. Glue carrot and nine buttons onto picket for face.

5. Fray edges of remaining fabric piece; tie around picket for scarf.

6. Glue remaining buttons onto picket below scarf.

7. Glue branches to back of picket for arms.

11

SLEEPY SANTA

Our sleepy crescent Santa lends unique charm to any door! He's made using simple felt shapes, and lamb's wool adds a soft touch to his cap. A sprig of faux holly leaves and berries finishes this "ho-ho-homemade" decoration.

WHAT TO BUY

$\frac{1}{8}$ yd. of artificial lamb's wool; $\frac{2}{3}$ yd. of red felt; $\frac{1}{3}$ yd. of ecru felt; tan felt piece; ecru, red, and black embroidery floss; and a small artificial holly pick

THINGS YOU HAVE AT HOME

Tracing paper, newspaper, 22" square of corrugated cardboard, craft knife, fabric marking pencil, pins, embroidery needle, craft glue, wire cutters, floral wire, and a hot glue gun

CRESCENT SANTA DOOR DECORATION

Before beginning project, refer to Embroidery Stitches, page 189. Use three strands of floss for all stitching. Use craft glue for all gluing unless otherwise indicated.

1. Trace patterns, page 163, onto tracing paper; cut out. Using patterns, cut pom-pom and hat trim from lamb's wool and face from tan felt.

2. Use black floss to work Backstitch and Straight Stitch for eye and eyelashes.

3. Refer to *Cutting a Fabric Circle*, page 191, to cut 18" and 12" dia. circle patterns from newspaper.

4. Draw around 18" circle pattern on cardboard. Position 12" circle pattern $\frac{1}{4}$" from edge of 18" circle (Fig. 1); draw around pattern.

Fig. 1

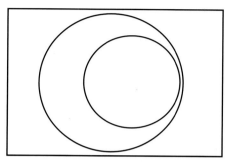

5. Position face, hat trim, and pom-pom patterns over drawn circles; draw around patterns on cardboard. Use craft knife to cut out cardboard shape as indicated by dashed lines in Fig. 2.

Fig. 2

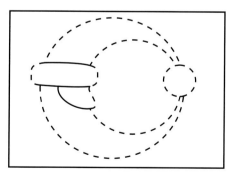

6. Position cardboard shape on red felt. Use fabric marking pen to draw around cardboard shape; cut out. Glue felt shape to front of cardboard shape.

7. For beard, draw around bottom half of crescent on ecru felt; cut out.

8. Arrange face, hat trim, pom-pom and beard on crescent; glue in place.

9. Use ecru floss to work Blanket Stitch around edges of beard and red floss to work Blanket Stitch around edges of hat.

10. Glue holly on hat trim.

11. For hanger, cut a 6" piece of floral wire; bend in half. Hot glue wire ends to back of crescent.

Display "heart-felt" wishes with this folksy wreath. Perky gingerbread men and jolly Santas make fun decorations for the wreath, which is made by tying strips of felt to a wire foundation.

WHAT TO BUY

1 yd. of green felt; one white, one flesh, one black, two tan, and three red felt pieces; red and black embroidery floss; six black beads; $1/2$ yd. of $5/8$"w red ribbon; white baby rickrack; and a 12" dia. wire wreath form

THINGS YOU HAVE AT HOME

Tracing paper, pinking shears, embroidery needle, paper-backed fusible web, thread, assorted small white buttons, wire cutters, floral wire, and a hot glue gun

JOLLY FELT WREATH

Refer to Embroidery Stitches, page 189, before beginning project. Use six strands of floss for all stitching.

1. Fuse both tan felt pieces together; fuse two red felt pieces together.

2. Trace Santa, boots, and gingerbread boy patterns, page 158, onto tracing paper; cut out. Draw around gingerbread boy pattern three times on fused tan felt and Santa pattern three times on fused red felt. Using boots pattern, cut three shapes from black felt. Cut out Santas. Use pinking shears to cut out gingerbread boys.

3. Carefully separate layers of felt at bottom of Santa body. Position boots between layers; pin in place.

4. Use black floss to work Blanket Stitch around edge of Santas, French Knots for eyes, and Straight Stitch for noses. Use red floss to work Backstitch for gingerbread boy mouths. Sew beads to gingerbread boys for eyes.

5. Follow *Fusing Basics*, page 187, and use patterns, page 158, to make three each of beard, mustache, pom-pom appliqués, and six cuff appliqués using pinking shears to cut out cuffs and pom-poms. Arrange appliqués on each Santa; fuse in place.

6. Cut three 19" lengths of rickrack. Hand sew one length to edge of each gingerbread boy. For bow ties, cut three 6" lengths of ribbon. Fold each length into a bow, wrapping red floss around center to secure; glue one bow to each figure.

7. Sew buttons on front of each figure.

8. For wreath, use pinking shears to cut green felt into 1" x 6" strips. Make a 1" lengthwise cut in center of each strip. Fold each strip around wire, pulling one end of strip through cut in center of strip (Fig. 1). Repeat with each strip until wreath form is covered.

Fig. 1

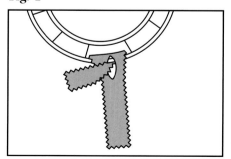

9. Cut six 5" lengths of floral wire. Glue center of wire to center back of each figure. Thread wire ends through wreath, twisting at back of wreath to secure.

10. For bow, use pinking shears and remaining red felt piece to cut two $1/2$" x 10" strips for loops, two $1/2$" x $4 1/2$" strips for streamers, and one 1" x $3 1/2$" strip for bow center. Cut a 1" x 8" strip. Wrap strip around top of wreath; overlap and glue ends in place. Assemble bow and glue together. Glue knot of bow to front of strip.

"Illuminated" Place Mats

Create cozy place settings at your Yuletide table with our soft, fleecy place mats. Each mat is "illuminated" with a string of light bulb appliqués and then edged with simple blanket stitching. A set of four also makes a great gift!

WHAT TO BUY
1/2 yd. of red thermal fleece; green yarn; yellow, green, blue, and black felt pieces; and yellow, green, blue, and black embroidery floss

THINGS YOU HAVE AT HOME
Yarn needle, tracing paper, embroidery needle, and thread

FLEECE PLACE MATS
Refer to Embroidery Stitches, page 189, before beginning project.

1. For four place mats, cut four 11 1/2" x 18 1/2" rectangles from fleece.

2. Use yarn needle and yarn to work Blanket Stitch around edge of each place mat.

3. Trace patterns, page 161, onto tracing paper; cut out. Using patterns, cut four bulbs each from yellow, green, and blue felt and twelve sockets from black felt.

4. For light string, arrange a 33" length of yarn on each place mat. Use thread to work Couching Stitch to secure yarn.

5. Arrange sockets and bulbs along light string. Use three strands of matching floss to work Blanket Stitch around edges of bulbs and sockets.

NO PEEKIN'!

*K*eep curious eyes from peeking at Santa's work with this petite door pillow. Trimming the bottom edge of the hanger, jingle bells are ready to sound the alarm that little ones are spying, hoping for a midnight glimpse!

WHAT TO BUY
Green and dark green felt pieces, red embroidery floss, ¹/₂ yd. of decorative cord, and nine 12mm gold jingle bells

THINGS YOU HAVE AT HOME
Tracing paper, embroidery needle, thread, three red buttons, and polyester fiberfill

"NO PEEKIN'" DOOR HANGER
Refer to Embroidery Stitches, page 189, before beginning project. Use six strands of floss for all stitching unless otherwise indicated.

1. Cut two 6" squares from green felt. Trace patterns, page 166, onto tracing paper. Using leaf pattern, cut four shapes from dark green felt.

2. Pin "No Peekin'" pattern onto one felt square. Stitching through pattern, work Couching Stitch, French Knot, and Straight Stitch to embroider words onto felt. Carefully tear away tracing paper.

3. Matching right sides and leaving an opening for stuffing, sew felt squares together. Clip corners and turn right side out. Sew leaves and buttons to top corner of pillow front. Stuff pillow with fiberfill; sew opening closed.

4. Tie a knot 1" from each end of cord; fray ends. Sew knots of cord to top corners of pillow.

5. Using three strands, thread needle with a 36" length of floss. For jingle bell fringe, secure floss at bottom corner of pillow. Bring needle through edge to front. Thread one bell onto floss. Bring needle through edge of pillow to form a ¹/₂" loop (Fig. 1). Bring needle around loop, catching floss under needle and tie a knot at top of loop (Fig. 2).

Fig. 1

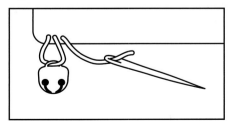

(Continued on page 149)

DINING ROOM DAZZLE

*Y*our table will truly sparkle when you dress it up with this extraordinary table runner. It's simple to cut motifs from Christmas fabric and fuse them to an inexpensive purchased runner. What an economical way to add dazzle to the dining room!

WHAT TO BUY
Table runner with tassels, ¼ yd. of poinsettia print Christmas fabric, and gold dimensional paint

THINGS YOU HAVE AT HOME
Paper-backed fusible web

POINSETTIA TABLE RUNNER
1. Fuse web to wrong side of fabric. Cut desired designs from fabric; fuse to each end of table runner.

2. Referring to *Painting Basics,* page 188, paint over edges of appliqués; allow to dry.

POSH POINSETTIA PILLOW

*T*his color-splashed accent commands attention! No one will guess that you simply dressed up one of your everyday throw pillows. The cover is easy to craft using floral print napkins and golden ribbon — and there's no sewing involved!

WHAT TO BUY
Two Christmas print 16$\frac{1}{2}$" square cloth napkins, one red 16$\frac{1}{2}$" square cloth napkin, and 3 yds. of $\frac{1}{4}$"w gold ribbon

THINGS YOU HAVE AT HOME
Square throw pillow (we used a 14" pillow) and seven safety pins

PILLOW COVER
1. Tie an 18" length of ribbon into a bow around the clasp edge of a pin. Tie another 18" ribbon into a bow around knot of first bow. Make three bow sets.

2. Overlapping edges of print napkins 1$\frac{3}{4}$", place wrong side up on a flat surface. Center pillow on napkins. Place red napkin over top of pillow. Bring ends

(Continued on page 147)

19

O HOLY NIGHT

You'll want to find a special place for this exquisite luminary! Using glass etching paint, silhouettes of the Holy Family are cast onto a simple hurricane globe. It will be a resplendent centerpiece for your holiday decor.

WHAT TO BUY
8¹/₂"h glass hurricane globe, clear self-adhesive vinyl shelf paper, white frost etching paint for glass, and a 4"h white candle

THINGS YOU HAVE AT HOME
Fine-point permanent pen; craft knife; clean, dry paintbrush; denatured alcohol; unused, smooth-textured sponge; and a tapestry needle

ETCHED NATIVITY GLOBE
1. Wash hurricane globe with soapy water; rinse and dry thoroughly. For ground portion of scene, cut a piece of shelf paper to fit around bottom half of globe. Cut a gentle wave pattern along top edge of paper piece; adhere to globe.

2. Use pen to trace pattern, page 155, onto vinyl side of a second piece of shelf paper. Remove paper backing and position on globe, slightly overlapping top edge of first paper piece. Use craft knife to carefully cut around designs; remove excess vinyl (background).

3. To condition globe, use paintbrush to apply alcohol to surface; allow to air dry.

4. Using sponge, follow manufacturer's instructions to apply etching paint over design on globe. Allow to dry for two hours; remove patterns. To create stars, halo, and star rays, use needle to scratch designs in etching paint.

5. Place candle inside globe.

IT'S "CHRISTMAS-THYME"

*O*ur *country Christmas angel will bring a touch of homespun charm to the kitchen. Because she's made with naturals and simple materials, you can craft her for next to nothing!*

WHAT TO BUY

¹/₃ yd. of muslin; yellow, red, green, and brown embroidery floss; and a small artificial bird

THINGS YOU HAVE AT HOME

Tracing paper, embroidery needle, thread, blush for cheeks, polyester fiberfill, a tapestry needle, three buttons, one 12" twig, two 8" twigs, two 8" cedar branches, jute twine, and a hot glue gun

CHRISTMAS KITCHEN ANGEL

Refer to Embroidery Stitches, page 189, before beginning project. Use six strands of floss for all stitching.

1. Trace patterns, page 153, onto tracing paper. Using head pattern, cut two shapes from muslin. Pin face pattern to one muslin shape. Stitching through pattern, work Running Stitch for eyebrows and nose and French Knots for eyes. Work Straight Stitch for mouth; carefully tear away pattern. Apply blush to cheeks.

2. Matching right sides and leaving neck open for stuffing, sew head shapes together; turn right side out. Stuff head with fiberfill; sew opening closed.

(Continued on page 147)

HANGIN' AROUND

*L*et this frosty fellow hang around
your kitchen! Our friendly snowman
hanger is easy to sew from felt and
attach to an ordinary dish towel. He'll
be a jolly — and useful — accent!

WHAT TO BUY

15½" x 16" kitchen towel; one blue, one
orange, two white, and two red felt pieces;
orange, blue, and black embroidery floss;
two ¾" dia. black shank buttons; and
1 yd. of ⅝"w red grosgrain ribbon

THINGS YOU HAVE AT HOME

Thread, tracing paper, batting, six
assorted black buttons, clear nylon
thread, and an embroidery needle

SNOWMAN DISH TOWEL

*Refer to Embroidery Stitches, page 189,
before beginning project. Use three
strands of floss for all stitching.*

1. Baste along one short end of towel;
pull thread to gather towel edge to
measure 5½". Knot thread ends and
adjust gathers evenly.

2. Trace patterns, page 169, onto tracing
paper. Using patterns, cut one nose from
orange felt, two heads from white felt, two
hatbands from blue felt, and two hats
from red felt. Cut one hat and one head
from batting.

3. Sew shank buttons for eyes and
assorted black buttons for mouth to one

head shape. Pin nose in place; use orange
floss to work Blanket Stitch around edges
of nose.

4. Pin hatbands to hat shapes. Using blue
floss, work Blanket Stitch along edges
of hatbands.

5. Position batting shapes between head
and hat shapes and gathered end of towel
between layers at bottom of head.

6. Cut ribbon in half. Position one end of
each ribbon piece between layers at top of
hat; pin in place.

7. Use clear nylon thread to machine
stitch through all layers around edges of
head and hat.

8. Tie ribbons into a bow.

PLACE MAT PILLOW

It's a snap to create a home accent that's super budget-friendly! Using ready-made place mats featuring holiday motifs, you can quickly stitch together this comfy throw pillow. It'll look great in any nook or cranny!

WHAT TO BUY
Two Christmas tapestry place mats and polyester fiberfill

THINGS YOU HAVE AT HOME
Thread

TAPESTRY PILLOW
1. Matching wrong sides and leaving an opening for stuffing, sew place mats together.

2. Stuff with fiberfill; sew opening closed.

23

SHADES OF CHRISTMAS

*D*ress up ordinary candlestick lamps for the holidays with these fabric-covered lampshades. You can choose from two festive finishes — miniature ornaments or an elegant gold bow. What a quick and inexpensive way to sprinkle a little Christmas cheer around your home!

WHAT TO BUY
Ornament Shade:
3" x 4¹/₂" x 5" lampshade, ¹/₄ yd. of fabric, twelve 15mm plastic Christmas ball ornaments, and ³/₄ yd. of ¹/₈"w gold cord

Bow Shade:
3" x 4¹/₂" x 5" lampshade, ¹/₄ yd. of fabric, ³/₄ yd. of 1¹/₂"w gold ribbon, and ³/₄ yd. of ¹/₄"w gold trim

THINGS YOU HAVE AT HOME
Tissue paper, tape, spray adhesive, gold thread, craft glue, and a hot glue gun

CHRISTMAS LAMPSHADES
1. Follow *Covering a Lampshade,* page 188, to cover each shade with fabric.

2. For ornament lampshade, thread one 3" length of gold thread through loop of each ornament. Spacing ornaments evenly, hot glue thread ends inside bottom of lampshade. Beginning and ending at seam of fabric, use craft glue to glue cord around top and bottom of shade.

3. For bow shade, glue trim around top and bottom of shade. Tie ribbon into a bow around shade; use hot glue to secure.

WINTRY WHIMSY

A whimsical orange nose and a bow-tied top hat make this fun fellow a great way to dress up the mantel! Inexpensive corduroy and flannel give the stocking a cuddly look — as well as an attractive price.

WHAT TO BUY
$3/8$ yd. of ecru corduroy, $1/4$ yd. of black corduroy, $1/8$ of flannel, two $5/8"$ dia. black buttons, five $1/2"$ dia. black buttons, and orange bump chenille stems

THINGS YOU HAVE AT HOME
Tracing paper; white, orange, and black thread; and a pencil

CORDUROY SNOWMAN STOCKING

Use a $1/4"$ seam allowance for all sewing unless otherwise indicated.

1. Trace patterns, page 156, onto tracing paper. Using patterns, cut two stocking shapes (one in reverse) from ecru corduroy and two hat shapes from black corduroy.

2. Matching right sides, sew stocking front and back together. Clip seams along curves; turn right side out.

3. Matching right sides, sew side edges of hat together; clip corners. Turn bottom edge of hat $1/4"$ to wrong side; stitch in place. Turn hat right side out.

4. To attach hat to stocking, place hat inside stocking, matching right side of hat to wrong side of stocking and matching top edges and side seams. Stitch together along top edges; turn hat out over stocking.

5. Sew $5/8"$ dia. buttons to stocking for eyes and $1/2"$ dia. buttons to stocking for mouth. For nose, curl chenille stem around a pencil; use orange thread to sew in place on snowman face.

(Continued on page 147)

25

HAPPY HOLIDAY FRIEND

Folks are sure to warm up to this happy homespun snowman. Made of corduroy and tied with a flannel scarf, our country accent will complement your decor — and your budget!

WHAT TO BUY

$1/2$ yd. of ecru corduroy, polyester fiberfill, orange felt piece, and black embroidery floss

THINGS YOU HAVE AT HOME

Thread, resealable sandwich bag, gravel or sand, 10" long twig, rubber band, drawing compass, tracing paper, two $5/8$" dia. black buttons, thread, embroidery needle, scrap of fabric for scarf, three assorted buttons, and a hot glue gun

COUNTRY CORDUROY SNOWMAN

1. For snowman body, cut a 16" x 22" rectangle from corduroy. Matching right sides and short edges, fold rectangle in half. Using a $1/2$" seam allowance, sew along side and one end of body; turn right side out. For arms, cut a small hole in each side of body.

2. Fill sandwich bag half full with gravel; seal bag. Place bag in bottom of snowman body. Insert twig through holes for arms. Stuff body with fiberfill to within 3" from top. Wrap rubber band around top 3" of body; adjust gathers evenly.

3. Use compass and tracing paper to make a $4^{1}/_{2}$" dia. circle pattern for snowman head. Trace snowman nose pattern, page 154, onto tracing paper. Using patterns, cut two heads from corduroy and one nose from felt.

4. Matching long edges, fold nose in half. Use floss to sew long edges together; stuff nose with fiberfill. For face, sew nose and $5/8$" black buttons for eyes to one head piece. Use floss and work Straight Stitch, page 189, to stitch mouth.

5. Matching wrong sides and leaving an opening for stuffing, use floss to whipstitch head pieces together. Stuff with fiberfill; sew opening closed. For "hair," pull a few strands of fiberfill to outside between stitching. Glue head to gathers at top of body.

6. Pull a small amount of fiberfill to outside of body at each arm opening.

7. For scarf, tear a $2^{1}/_{2}$" x 15" strip of fabric; knot around neck over rubber band.

8. Knotting ends at front of buttons and leaving long tails, use floss to sew remaining buttons to front of snowman.

HOLLY-BRIGHT TREE SKIRT

*Y*ou can add spirit to your holiday decor with our bright holly-trimmed tree skirt! Vibrant red corduroy and green felt come together to create an eye-catching Christmas decoration that you'll enjoy year after year.

WHAT TO BUY

Three green and three dark green felt pieces, 1⅛ yds. of red corduroy, and three skeins of green embroidery floss

THINGS YOU HAVE AT HOME

Tracing paper, pinking shears, pencil, string, thumbtack, ½"w paper-backed fusible web tape, scraps of four different green fabrics, thread, and fabric glue

HOLLY TREE SKIRT

1. Trace patterns, page 155, onto tracing paper. Using leaf patterns, cut nine A's from dark green felt. Use pinking shears to cut nine B's from green felt. Center one A on each B and glue in place. Cut 23 C's from dark green felt. Use pinking shears to cut 23 D's from green felt. Center one C on each D and glue in place.

(Continued on page 148)

YULETIDE GREETINGS

*W*hat a creative way to display all the greeting cards we receive during the Yuletide! Use mini clothespins to clip cards to a ribbon "clothesline" held up by two happy gingerbread men.

WHAT TO BUY

$1/2$ yd. of fabric for background and hanging sleeve, $1/4$ yd. of fabric for border, $1/4$ yd. of fabric for binding, two wooden heart buttons, $1^1/2$"h alphabet stencil, 1 yd. of $1/8$"w red ribbon, mini clothespins, and a $3/8$" dia. wooden dowel

THINGS YOU HAVE AT HOME

Heavyweight fusible interfacing; paper-backed fusible web; scraps of Christmas print fabrics, tan fabric, red fabric, and white felt; $3/4$"w paper-backed fusible web tape; pinking shears; red and black embroidery floss; $1/4$" dia. hole punch; craft glue; paintbrush; red acrylic paint; two $3/4$" dia. buttons; and a pencil

CHRISTMAS CARD WALL HANGING

Refer to Embroidery Stitches, page 189, before beginning project. Use six strands of floss for all stitching.

1. For background, cut $12^1/2$" x 34" rectangles from fabric and interfacing. Fuse interfacing to wrong side of fabric.

2. For border, cut two $2^1/4$" x 34" and two $2^1/4$" x $12^1/2$" strips from fabric and fusible web. Fuse long strips to top and bottom and short strips to sides of background.

3. Follow *Fusing Basics*, page 187, to make four $2^1/4$" square appliqués from Christmas fabric; fuse one square to each corner of border.

4. For binding, cut two 2" x $13^1/2$" and two 2" x 34" strips from fabric. Press long edges of 34" strips $1/4$" to wrong side. Press short edges of $13^1/2$" strips $1/2$" to wrong side and long edges $1/4$" to wrong side. Fuse web tape to wrong sides of binding strips. Centering edges of background between folds, fuse top and bottom binding strips, then side binding strips to background.

(Continued on page 149)

SANTA'S PATHWAY

*H*ere's a fun idea for adding holiday spirit to your lawn. We used acrylic paint to decorate an inexpensive stepping stone. Why not make enough to create a path for Santa to follow to your door!

WHAT TO BUY
One 12" dia. concrete garden stone and white, flesh, red, and black acrylic paint

THINGS YOU HAVE AT HOME
Tracing paper, paintbrushes, black medium-point felt-tip marker, and clear acrylic spray sealer

GARDEN STONE SANTA

Allow paint to dry after each color application.

1. Referring to *Making Patterns,* page 187, trace patterns, page 152, onto tracing paper; cut out. Draw around patterns on garden stone, overlapping as necessary.

2. Paint designs. Mix small amounts of red and white paint together to paint Santa's nose, cheeks, and mouth. Use white paint to add highlights.

3. Use marker to add details to Santa and candy cane stripes on "HO HO HO."

4. Spray design with two or three coats of acrylic sealer.

REDWORK CHARM

Bring back the old-fashioned style of redwork embroidery with these amazingly economical stockings. A Battenberg lace cuff stitched with a merry message adds antique charm to these mantel decorations.

WHAT TO BUY
1/2 yd. of fabric, 8" x 12" oval Battenberg doily, and red embroidery floss

THINGS YOU HAVE AT HOME
Tracing paper, transfer paper, thread, and embroidery needle

REDWORK STOCKINGS
Refer to Embroidery Stitches, page 189, before beginning project. Use two strands of floss for all stitching.

1. Referring to *Making Patterns*, page 187, trace stocking pattern, page 164, onto tracing paper. Using pattern, cut stocking front and back from fabric.

2. Matching right sides and leaving top edge open, use a 1/4" seam allowance to sew stocking front and back together. Clip curves; turn stocking right side out and press. Turn top edge of stocking 1/2" to inside; press. Turn pressed edge 1/2" again and press. Sew around top of stocking 1/4" below top edge.

3. For hanger, cut a 3" x 12" strip of fabric. Turn long edges of strip 3/4" to wrong side; press. Matching turned

edges, fold strip in half lengthwise; press. Sew along double folded edges. Fold strip in half to form a loop. Sew ends inside top of stocking at back seam.

4. Matching short ends, fold doily in half; cut doily along fold. Trace embroidery pattern, page 165, onto tracing paper. Transfer pattern onto right side of one doily half.

5. Embroider design using Stem Stitch, Backstitch, Lazy Daisy Stitch, and French Knot.

6. Match right side raw edge of doily to wrong side top edge of stocking front; sew in place. Turn doily out over front of stocking; press.

EASY KITCHEN ACCENT

*S*tart your holiday decorating from the ground up with this easy no-sew floorcloth! Fusing simple fabric cutouts to a plain purchased mat creates a great Christmas decoration that's useful, too.

WHAT TO BUY
20" x 34" half-round canvas floorcloth and ⅛ yd. each of red and green fabrics

THINGS YOU HAVE AT HOME
Paper-backed fusible web

APPLIQUÉD FLOORCLOTH
1. Follow *Fusing Basics*, page 187, and use patterns, page 159 , to make bow, bow center, holly, and berry appliqués from fabrics.

2. Cut 1¼" x 38" strips from fabric and fusible web; fuse together. Cut strip into 2" lengths.

3. Arrange appliqués and strips on floorcloth; fuse in place.

ONE-HOUR DECORATING

Celebrate this holiday season in a very special way — by filling your home with clever handmade decorations created in less than one hour! Spruce up your kitchen with a rustic tree-trimmed towel, or accent your mantel with a quick-to-fix tasseled swag. You can also perk up a quiet corner with a holiday button-embellished frame, top your table with elegant place mats, and much more. When you see the exciting ideas in this section, you'll want to start planning a holly-jolly holiday right away!

SPICED CANDLE

*O*ur *homey candle has aromatic appeal! It's created by rolling a wax-dipped pillar candle in seasonings you'll find in your pantry. Taking only a half-hour to make, this rustic illuminator is a lovely way to brighten a quiet corner.*

AROMATIC SPICED CANDLE

You will need: coffee can, saucepan, newspaper, clear candle wax, black acrylic paint, foam paintbrush, 4" dia. tart pan, weathering paint for metal, 6"h pillar candle, aluminum foil, spices (we used nutmeg, allspice, and cinnamon), 1" x 18" torn fabric strip, cinnamon stick, and artificial greenery.

1. (**Caution**: Do not melt wax in saucepan placed directly on burner.) Cover work area with newspaper. Place enough wax in can to immerse candle. (Remember that melted wax will rise when candle is immersed.) Place can in saucepan; fill saucepan half full with water. Heat water until wax melts.

2. Thin black paint with a small amount of water. Referring to *Painting Basics* (pg. 188), use foam paintbrush to apply a thin coat of black paint to tart pan; allow to dry slightly.

3. Apply one coat of weathering paint over black paint; allow to dry.

4. Sprinkle desired spices on a 12" square of foil. Holding candle by wick, carefully immerse candle in melted wax; roll in spices. Repeat two more times; allow to harden.

5. Tie fabric strip into a bow around candle. Insert cinnamon stick and greenery behind bow.

IN ONLY
50
MINUTES!

Country charm goes into the making of this fun accent pillow! Torn strips of assorted green fabrics are machine-stitched together over a string and then clipped and gathered to create the shaggy wreath. Just glue the wreath to a ready-made pillow, then add buttons and a contrasting torn fabric bow for a festive finish!

FABRIC WREATH PILLOW
You will need: 4¹/₂" x 45" torn strips of three coordinating green fabrics, 48" length of string, green thread, 16" square pillow, 2¹/₂" x 26" torn fabric strip for bow, assorted red buttons, and a hot glue gun and glue sticks.

1. Stack green fabric strips together, wrong sides up.

2. Place string along center of fabric strips. Taking care to not stitch through string, use a wide zigzag stitch to sew over string.

3. Making cuts 1" apart, clip fabric up to but not through zigzag stitching on each side of string.

4. Pull string to gather fabric to a 24" length. Tie ends of string together, forming a loop; trim excess string.

5. Center wreath on pillow and glue in place.

6. Tie torn fabric strip into a bow; glue bow to bottom of wreath.

7. Glue buttons to wreath.

The holidays are a whirlwind of activities, and our illuminating snow fellow is just the thing to brighten them! With a little paint, a scrap of flannel fabric, and a candle, you can give heartwarming appeal to an ordinary hurricane globe.

HURRICANE SNOWMAN

You will need: sponge piece; paintbrushes; white, orange, green, and black enamel glass paints; glass hurricane globe; tracing paper; and a 1" x 20" flannel strip.

1. Referring to *Painting Basics* (pg. 188), use sponge piece to stamp white paint on hurricane globe; allow to dry.

2. Trace mitten pattern (pg. 176) onto tracing paper; cut out. Draw around pattern on globe, reversing for opposite hand.

3. Use green paint to paint mittens.

4. Use black paint to paint eyes, mouth, and buttons on snowman and cuffs on mittens. Use white paint to highlight eyes and buttons.

5. Use orange paint to paint nose on snowman; use black paint to add details to nose.

6. For scarf fringe, make clips in ends of flannel strip; tie scarf into a knot around globe.

*Y*ou can bring the enticing scent of country spice into your home with our clove-studded candles. These stunning wax creations are a breeze to make by embellishing pillar candles with cloves, pinecones, and anise stars.

CLOVE-STUDDED CANDLES

You will need: gold spray paint, two 3$^1/_2$" dia. jar lids, drawing compass, corrugated cardboard, black pen, disposable lighter, whole cloves, whole anise stars, preserved pine greenery, miniature pinecones, metallic gold acrylic paint, small paintbrush, and a hot glue gun and glue sticks.

For tall candle, you will also need: 3"dia. x 6"h white candle and pinecone roses.

For short candle, you will also need: 3"dia. x 3"h white candle.

1. Apply one coat of gold spray paint to jar lids; allow to dry.

2. Use compass to draw two 4$^1/_2$" dia. circles on cardboard; cut out.

3. Center one jar lid right side up on each cardboard circle; draw around lid on cardboard. Apply glue to drawn circle; press rim of lid into glue. Place one candle in each jar lid and glue in place; allow to dry.

4. Use pen to place dots on candles for clove placement. Heat point of compass over flame of lighter and insert point into each dot to melt wax slightly.

5. Trim each clove stem so that $^1/_8$" of stem remains. Place a dot of glue on end of each stem, then quickly insert clove into hole in candle.

6. For each candle, cut several 4" lengths of greenery. Glue greenery around edge of cardboard circle, overlapping as needed.

7. For tall candle, glue three pinecone roses and two miniature pinecones onto greenery at base of candle. Use gold acrylic paint to highlight cloves, roses, and pinecones.

8. For short candle, glue six anise stars and six miniature pinecones onto greenery at base of candle. Use gold acrylic paint to highlight anise stars, pinecones, and cloves.

*C*raft a colorful decoration to brighten a holiday spot — the tree, the mantle, or an evergreen garland — in less than a half-hour! For this versatile accent, simply glue fanciful heart and snowman cutouts onto a length of festive wooden beads.

SNOWMAN GARLAND

You will need: tracing paper, white and red craft foam, scrap of orange felt, black dimensional paint, four $^1/_2$" dia. green buttons, 60" length of wooden bead garland, and a hot glue gun and glue sticks.

1. Trace snowman head, bow tie, nose, and heart patterns (pg. 177) onto tracing paper; cut out. Use patterns to cut three heads, three bow ties, and four hearts from craft foam and three noses from felt.

2. For each snowman, glue bow tie and nose to head. Referring to *Painting*

Basics (pg. 188), use dimensional paint to paint face on snowman.

3. Glue one button to center of each heart.

4. Remove all but twelve beads from garland. Glue back of one heart to string next to twelfth bead. Add twelve more beads to string; glue back of one snowman to string next to twelfth bead. Continue, alternating snowmen and hearts every twelve beads, until all snowmen and hearts are used. Add twelve more beads to string; tie end of string in a knot to secure.

Holiday drop-ins will "chill out" in a hurry at the sight of this cool Yule greeting! Dressed in a top hat and bright ribbon scarf, this handsome snowman is a breeze to create from craft foam to dress up a simple pine wreath. Add buttons, snowflakes, red ball ornaments, and sprigs of holly to complete your wintry welcome.

SNOWMAN WREATH

You will need: tracing paper; white, orange, and black craft foam; $4^3/4$" length of $1/4$"w ribbon; one stem of small artificial holly leaves; two $1/2$" dia. black buttons; three $6^1/2$" dia. snowflake ornaments; three $1/2$" dia. red buttons; black permanent felt-tip marker; nine small red glass ball ornaments; six large stems of artificial holly leaves with berries; 20" dia. pine wreath; 2 yds. of $1^1/2$"w ribbon; and a hot glue gun and glue sticks.

1. Trace snowman head, hat, and nose patterns (pg. 175) onto tracing paper; cut out. Use patterns to cut one hat from black craft foam, one head from white craft foam, and one nose from orange craft foam.

2. Glue $1/4$"w ribbon and small holly sprig in place on hat. Glue hat and nose to snowman head. Glue black buttons for eyes to snowman head; use marker to draw mouth.

3. For each snowflake center, remove five small holly leaves from stem. Arrange leaves and glue to center of snowflake. Glue a red button to center of leaves.

4. Arrange large holly stems, snowflake ornaments, glass ball ornaments, and snowman on wreath; glue in place.

5. For scarf, glue ribbon under snowman head and arrange streamers on wreath; glue in place.

6. For scarf fringe, make 1" clips in ribbon ends.

*I*n the blink of an eye, you can create a striking centerpiece! Glue silk flowers and leaves along the edge of a basket and then fill it with natural accents.

POINSETTIA BASKET
You will need: poinsettia bush (ours had 14 flowers), 18" long oblong wicker basket, and a hot glue gun and glue sticks.

1. Remove flowers and leaves from poinsettia bush.

2. Glue flowers and leaves along top edge of basket.

*S*urprise the bird-watcher in your family with a delightful decorative birdhouse. To save time, the wooden house and star accents are allowed to dry while the tiny tree and evergreen "shingles" are prepared. With all the trims glued in place, the tabletop display is nested in a tuft of Spanish moss.

HOLIDAY BIRDHOUSE

You will need: wood-tone spray; 8"h wooden birdhouse; four 1¹/₂"h wooden stars; yellow acrylic paint; paintbrush; 4¹/₂" x 6¹/₂" rectangles of fabric, poster board, and paper-backed fusible web; tracing paper; wire cutters; artificial pine greenery; black felt-tip pen; floral wire; pencil; small stem of artificial leaves with berries; Spanish moss; twigs; and a hot glue gun and glue sticks.

1. Apply wood-tone spray to birdhouse; paint wooden stars yellow. Allow paint to dry.

2. Referring to *Fusing Basics* (pg. 187), use web to fuse fabric and poster board rectangles together.

3. Trace birdhouse tree pattern (pg. 174) onto tracing paper; cut out. Draw around tree pattern on poster board side of rectangle; cut out.

4. Measure one side of roof from top to bottom. Use wire cutters to cut twelve pieces of pine greenery the determined length. Glue six pieces to each side of roof.

5. Use pen to draw "stitches" on stars. Use wire cutters to cut three 6" lengths of floral wire; wrap around pencil to curl. Glue one wire length to back of each of three stars; glue ends of wires to roof.

6. Glue remaining star to top of tree. Glue tree to front of birdhouse.

7. Use wire cutters to cut three sprigs of leaves and berries from stem. Glue twigs and two sprigs to birdhouse roof; glue remaining sprig to tree.

8. Arrange Spanish moss around base and in openings of birdhouse; glue in place.

*O*ur wintry white Father Christmas provides a nostalgic focal point for a Yuletide arrangement. His kindly face can be cut from gift wrap or an old greeting card, and he sports a long beard of curly craft hair. His body takes shape fast by covering a foam cone with cotton batting and fur trim.

FATHER CHRISTMAS

You will need: cotton batting, ¹/₈ yd. of artificial lamb's wool, tracing paper, 9" x 3⁷/₈" foam cone, gift wrap or card with Santa face, 2" length of 1" dia. foam tube, 3" length of craft hair, 12" length of floral wire, small piece of artificial greenery with pinecone, and a hot glue gun and glue sticks.

1. From batting, cut one 9" x 13¹/₂" piece for coat and one 3" x 10" piece for sleeves.

2. From lamb's wool, cut one 3¹/₂" square for hood, one ³/₄" x 7¹/₂" strip for coat front, one ³/₄" x 14" strip for bottom of coat, and two ³/₄" x 3¹/₂" strips for cuffs.

3. Trace mitten pattern (pg. 176) onto tracing paper. Use pattern to cut four shapes from batting.

4. Overlapping ¹/₄", glue short edges of batting piece for coat together, forming a tube. Place coat over cone. With glued seam at center front, gather top of coat around cone and secure with floral wire.

5. Glue ³/₄" x 14" wool trim around bottom of coat. Glue ³/₄" x 7¹/₂" wool trim down center front of coat, covering seam.

6. For head, cut face from gift wrap or card; glue face to foam tube. Cut a 1¹/₂" length of craft hair; glue to face for beard. Follow craft hair manufacturer's instructions to fluff beard. Glue head to top of body.

7. Fold lamb's wool square for hood in half, wrong sides together. Glue one short end together. Place over head and glue to secure.

8. For arms, glue 1¹/₂" of each end of floral wire between two mitten shapes. Place arm wire along center of batting piece for sleeves. Place dots of glue over wire to secure. Glue long edges of sleeves together. Glue wool trim for cuff around each sleeve end.

9. Glue center of arms to back of body just below hat; bend arms to front of body.

10. Glue greenery to one hand.

CHARMING STOCKING

Turn on the charm with this elegant gold-trimmed stocking. Braid is glued to a ready-made stocking in a stylized Christmas tree design, and heart-shaped charms serve as "ornaments." Santa is sure to fill this lavish sock with lots of goodies!

HEART CHARM STOCKING
You will need: tracing paper, iron-on transfer pen, ecru stocking, gold braid trim, assorted heart-shaped charms, and a hot glue gun and glue sticks.

1. Use tracing paper and transfer pen to make ribbon tree pattern (pg. 176). Follow pen manufacturer's instructions to transfer pattern to stocking front.

2. Glue gold trim onto stocking over transferred tree design.

3. Arrange charms on tree and glue in place.

Welcome winter with our happy-go-lucky snowman and his little bird buddy! The jolly fellow is fashioned using sock-covered foam balls, then "dressed" in cheery checked fabric and bright red felt.

BIRD-IN-HAND SNOWMAN

You will need: serrated knife, two 3" dia. foam balls, one 2" dia. foam ball, heavy gauge floral wire, wire cutters, 17" square of polyester batting, rubber band, white sock, tracing paper, 1/2" x 7" strip of white felt, scrap of yellow felt, black felt-tip pen, pinking shears, 3 1/2" x 11 1/2" rectangle of red felt for pants, drawing compass, two 1/4" x 7" strips of red felt for suspenders, straight pins, 20mm white pom-pom, 1" x 16" torn fabric strip, orange and black dimensional paint, two straight pins with black bead heads, two small black buttons, two small white buttons, two small twigs, black embroidery floss, and a hot glue gun and glue sticks.

1. For base of snowman, use serrated knife to cut one 3" foam ball in half.

2. Stack remaining 3" ball and 2" ball on rounded side of base. Insert floral wire through center of stack; use wire cutters to clip wire end even with top of small ball.

3. Center batting over top of snowman and smooth around head; wrap rubber band around bottom of head. Continue to smooth batting over snowman body. Trim batting even with bottom of base.

4. Pull sock snugly over snowman. Apply glue around edge of base bottom. Press sock into glue; allow to dry. Trim away excess sock.

5. Trace hat and bird patterns (pg. 178) onto tracing paper. Use patterns to cut one hat from red felt and one bird from yellow felt. Use pen to draw details on bird.

6. Overlapping 1/4", glue straight edges of hat together. For hat trim, use pinking shears to cut along one long edge of 1/2" x 7" strip of white felt. Matching straight edge of trim to bottom edge of hat, glue trim to hat.

7. Extending felt 1/2" past bottom edge of base of snowman, wrap felt for pants around snowman body; glue in place. Fold excess fabric under and glue to bottom of base.

8. Use drawing compass and tracing paper to make a 3" dia. pattern; cut one shape from red felt. Glue shape to bottom of snowman.

9. Spacing 1 1/2" apart, tuck one end of each suspender into front of pants; glue in place. Wrap suspenders over snowman shoulders, crisscrossing at back. Glue remaining ends of suspenders into back of pants.

10. Place hat on snowman head. Use straight pins to hold in place. Fold point of hat over and insert straight pin to scrunch hat down. Glue pom-pom over head of straight pin.

11. For patch, tear a 1" square from one end of fabric strip; glue to pants.

12. Referring to *Painting Basics* (pg. 188), use black paint to paint mouth and draw "stitches" on suspenders, pants, and patch. Apply small dots of orange paint for snowman nose and bird beak. For eyes, insert beaded straight pins into head.

13. Glue black buttons to snowman chest, and white buttons below front suspenders.

14. For arms, insert ends of twigs into sides of snowman body. Glue bird to one arm.

15. Tie scarf around snowman neck. Tie a 10" length of embroidery floss into a bow; glue to front of pants.

This sweet stocking will be ready to hold lots of Santa's goodies on Christmas Eve! We used a ready-made stocking to save time. The cheery motifs are quickly glued in place, along with the contrasting buttons and rickrack.

GINGER GIRL STOCKING

You will need: 14" canvas stocking, red jumbo rickrack, tracing paper, craft knife, yellow foam meat tray, floral wood-tone spray, red felt piece, two 5mm white pom-poms, white baby rickrack, nine white buttons, 12" length of 1"w grosgrain ribbon, and tacky glue.

1. Measure around top and toe of stocking; cut a length of jumbo rickrack for each measurement. Glue each rickrack length to stocking.

2. Trace body, cheek, foot, and heart patterns (pg. 179) onto tracing paper; cut out. Use craft knife to cut one body shape from foam tray. Cut two each of cheek and foot shapes and one heart from felt.

3. Spray body with wood-tone spray; allow to dry. Glue felt cutouts and pom-poms for eyes to body.

4. Trimming to fit, glue white rickrack across arms and legs, along neck, and around top of head. Glue a small piece of white rickrack to face for mouth.

5. Glue ginger girl to stocking.

6. Glue buttons to ginger girl and stocking.

7. Tie ribbon into a bow; glue to head.

*B*ring an extra measure of cheer to your home with this "merry" greeting. It's created with purchased wooden letters that are painted and glued inside star-shaped cookie cutters. Torn-fabric bows tie it all together.

"BE MERRY" STARS

You will need: red and green acrylic paint, paintbrushes, 1³/₄"h wooden letter cutouts to spell BE MERRY, white dimensional paint, seven 1" x 7" torn fabric strips, seven 3"w star-shaped metal cookie cutters, and a hot glue gun and glue sticks.

1. Apply one coat of red paint to letters that spell the word MERRY; allow to dry.

2. Apply one coat of green paint to letters that spell the word BE; allow to dry.

3. Referring to *Painting Basics* (pg. 188), use dimensional paint to apply dots to all letters.

4. Use torn fabric strips to tie five cookie cutters together and to tie a bow to cookie cutter at each end. Tie remaining two cookie cutters together. Insert letters into cookie cutters to spell words; glue in place.

*O*ur Christmas tree towel gets its charming homespun look from a mixture of fabric scraps. Fusible web appliqués and machine stitching make this towel surprisingly quick to assemble.

CHRISTMAS TREE KITCHEN TOWEL
You will need: 7" x 10" and 6" x 9" fabric rectangles, paper-backed fusible web, scraps of assorted fabrics for appliqués, clear nylon thread, kitchen towel, red embroidery floss, and four ¹/₂" dia. red buttons.

1. Press edges of both fabric rectangles ¹/₂" to wrong side. Center smaller rectangle on larger rectangle; topstitch in place along pressed edges.

2. Referring to *Fusing Basics* (pg. 187), use tree bottom, tree top, tree trunk, and tree topper patterns (pg. 180) to make appliqués from fabric scraps. Arrange appliqués on center of fabric rectangles and fuse in place. Use a narrow zigzag stitch and clear nylon thread to stitch over edges of appliqués.

3. Position rectangle on towel; topstitch in place along outer edges.

4. Use embroidery floss to sew one button to each corner of large rectangle.

OLDE SANTA BASKET

IN ONLY 30 MINUTES!

Sweet-smelling spices, a nostalgic greeting card, and perky checked fabric transform an ordinary basket into a pretty decoration. Equipped with a hot glue gun and pinking shears, you can assemble this lovely container in 30 minutes flat!

RUSTIC BASKET

You will need: pinking shears; 5" squares of checked fabric, paper-backed fusible web, and poster board; woven basket at least 6 1/4"h from bottom to rim; Christmas card; 5/8"w green grosgrain ribbon; two whole anise stars; cinnamon sticks; miniature pinecones; dried apple slice; dried cranberries; sprig of artificial pine greenery; and a hot glue gun and glue sticks.

1. Referring to *Fusing Basics* (pg. 187), use web to fuse fabric and poster board together. Pink edges of fused square.

2. Cut desired motif from card. Center motif on fabric square; glue in place. Center square on front of basket; glue in place.

3. Measure around rim of basket; add 1". Cut a length of ribbon the determined measurement. Overlapping ends at center front of basket, glue ribbon around rim. Cut a 30" length of ribbon. Tie ribbon into a double-loop bow and glue to ribbon at front of basket. Glue one anise star to knot of bow.

4. Arrange remaining anise star, dried fruit, cinnamon sticks, pinecones, and greenery over one corner of fabric square; glue in place.

49

IN ONLY
4'5
MINUTES!

*I*nfant socks and fabric scraps provide an easy way to trim this star-studded string. Patches fused to the tea-dyed "stockings" and cinnamon sticks laced onto the garland add to the country appeal.

STOCKING SWAG
You will need: paper-backed fusible web, scraps of assorted fabrics, infant-size white socks, tea dye bath, cinnamon sticks, black medium-point marker, 2" dia. wooden star cutouts, 3/4" dia. green buttons, craft wire, twelve 15mm red wooden beads, mini clothespins, and a hot glue gun and glue sticks.

1. Referring to *Fusing Basics* (pg. 187), use heel and toe patterns (pg. 179) to make appliqués. Arrange appliqués on socks and fuse in place.

2. Follow dye manufacturer's instructions to dye socks.

3. Cut six 4" lengths from cinnamon sticks.

4. Tear eighteen 1" x 8" strips from assorted fabrics. Knot three strips around center of each cinnamon stick.

5. Use marker to draw "stitches" on stars. Glue one button to center of each star; glue one star to center of each cinnamon stick.

6. Cut a 60" length of craft wire. Arrange swag as follows: one bead, one cinnamon stick, one bead; repeat order until all cinnamon sticks and beads are used, ending with one bead. Use a clothespin to attach each sock to wire between two beads.

IN ONLY 3 2 MINUTES!

*N*ovelty buttons, painted in bright Christmasy hues, add a festive touch to a plain wooden frame. Just thread the stars, hearts, and trees onto a length of embroidery floss and glue them around the edges. It's a great spot to show off a photo of the star of the family!

BUTTON FRAME

You will need: small wooden star, heart, and tree buttons; yellow, red, and green acrylic paint; paintbrushes; white embroidery floss; needle; 5" x 7" wooden frame; and glue.

1. Paint buttons desired colors; allow to dry.

2. Thread buttons onto a 36" length of floss; knot ends of floss together.

3. Arrange buttons around frame and glue in place.

*Y*ou can add luster to a velvet pillow in less time than it takes Santa to settle his sleigh on your rooftop! Sew two fabric napkins together, arrange them around the pillow, gather the ends with a rubber band, and finish with a tasseled gold cord!

HOLIDAY PILLOW

You will need: two 18" square metallic gold cloth napkins, 12" x 16" green velvet pillow, rubber band, and a 13" long gold cord with tasseled ends.

1. Using a ¹/₄" seam allowance, sew napkins together along one edge.

2. Wrap napkins around pillow and gather ends with rubber band; adjust gathers.

3. Tie cord around napkin ends, covering rubber band.

HANDSOME MANTEL SCARF

IN ONLY
30
MINUTES!

*O*ur no-sew tasseled holiday scarf
is a tasteful highlight for a handsome
mantelpiece. In only half an hour, you
can transform pretty cloth napkins into
an eye-catching accent.

CHRISTMAS MANTEL SCARF
You will need: one 17" square of paper-backed fusible web, three 17" square
fabric Christmas napkins, three gold
tassels, and a hot glue gun and
glue sticks.

1. Cut an 8^1/$_2$" square from one corner
of fusible web. Cut 8^1/$_2$" square in half
diagonally, making two triangles.

2. Referring to *Fusing Basics* (pg. 187),
fuse a web triangle to wrong side of one
corner (top) of each of two napkins. For
center piece of mantel scarf, fuse
remaining web piece to remaining
napkin. (This will leave an 8^1/$_2$" square of
this napkin free of web.)

3. Arrange napkins wrong side up as
shown in Fig. 1, positioning fused
sections at top of scarf.

Fig. 1

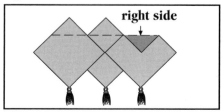

right side

4. Fold (indicated by dotted line) top
corners to wrong side of scarf and fuse
in place.

5. Glue hanging loop of one tassel to
wrong side of each lower point of
mantel scarf.

53

*O*ur bright and cheery banner is a colorful reminder of this joyous season. Vibrant silk poinsettia petals and leaves are fused to a canvas banner, then fabric pieces are added to create the flowerpot and topiary stem.

YULETIDE BANNER

You will need: 19^3/$_4$" x 27^1/$_2$" canvas banner with dowel and dowel caps, white spray paint, 23" long gold cord with tasseled ends, aluminum foil, paper-backed fusible web, silk poinsettia bush with five flowers, ^{1}/$_4$ yd. of Christmas fabric, 1"w fusible web tape, ^{3}/$_4$" x 6" rectangle of green fabric, 20" length of 2^1/$_2$"w gold wired ribbon, gold dimensional paint, and a hot glue gun and glue sticks.

Note: Refer to *Fusing Basics* (pg. 187) for Steps 2 through 6, following Foil Method for Step 3.

1. Use spray paint to paint dowel and dowel caps; allow to dry.

2. Cut two 1" x 27^1/$_2$" and two 1" x 19^3/$_4$" strips of Christmas fabric. Fuse web tape to wrong side of each strip. Arrange strips along edges of banner; fuse in place.

3. Remove leaves and petals from poinsettia bush. Fuse web to wrong sides of petals and leaves to make appliqués.

4. Use pattern (pg. 181) to make one flowerpot appliqué from Christmas fabric.

5. For stem appliqué, fuse web tape to wrong side of green fabric.

6. Arrange poinsettia, flowerpot, and stem appliqués on banner and fuse in place.

7. Tie ribbon into a bow; glue to top of flowerpot.

8. Referring to *Painting Basics* (pg. 188), use dimensional paint to apply dots at flower centers.

9. Tie one end of gold cord to each end of dowel.

*L*ooking for an elegant addition to your holiday table? Then this quick project is for you! Silk flower petals and leaves are removed from the stems and fused onto the corner of an ordinary place mat. Gold dimensional paint finishes the project with sparkle. Craft several to make a festive setting for your dinner guests.

POINSETTIA PLACE MAT
You will need: one white silk poinsettia with eight to ten petals, aluminum foil, paper-backed fusible web, red fabric place mat, and gold glitter dimensional paint.

1. Remove leaves and petals from poinsettia stem.

2. Referring to *Fusing Basics* (pg. 187), follow Foil Method to fuse web to wrong sides of poinsettia petals and leaves for appliqués.

3. Arrange appliqués on one corner of place mat; fuse in place.

4. Referring to *Painting Basics* (pg. 188), paint over edges of each appliqué; paint detail lines on petals and leaves.

Spice up your ornament collection or create wonderful little gifts with the exciting tree-trimmers on the following pages! Artists will appreciate the paintbrush Santas, while romantics will love the old-fashioned heart pocket. Your evergreen will command extra attention when you add glowing snowman light covers. Little felt elves create merry magic, and country angels and folk-art mittens add a touch of rustic charm. So don't spend your money on those expensive department-store trims — come craft with us!

57

MERRY MINI MITTENS

Warm and toasty, our mini mitten ornaments will add a wintry feel to your evergreen. Fused-on fabric scraps are used to create the folksy designs, which are accented with hand-stitched messages to complete the homestyle look.

WHAT TO BUY

Pair of miniature mittens and red embroidery floss

THINGS YOU HAVE AT HOME

Scraps of assorted fabrics, paper-backed fusible web, and a black permanent fine-point pen

MINI MITTEN ORNAMENTS

1. Follow *Fusing Basics*, page 187, and use patterns, page 159, to make tree, heart, star, leaf, and trunk appliqués from fabric scraps.

2. Arrange appliqués on mittens; fuse in place. Use pen to draw detail lines on leaves.

3. Use three strands of floss and work Backstitch, page 189, to stitch "Love" on one mitten cuff and "Joy" on remaining mitten cuff.

PEACEFUL TIDINGS

*W*ho better than an angel to watch over your family and friends? This country-style seraph begins as a wooden spoon, and delicate tea-dyed doilies provide her easy-to-make apron and wings. For a heavenly price, she'll spread peace to all who enter your holiday home.

WHAT TO BUY

17" long wooden spoon, two 12" dia. doilies, $1/3$ yd. of muslin, $1/8$"w green ribbon (10-yd. spool), $1/4$"w ecru ribbon (10-yd. spool), wool doll hair, and a sprig of artificial holly

THINGS YOU HAVE AT HOME

Two tea bags, five $5/8$" dia. buttons, black fine-point pen, red colored pencil, rubber band, 1" dia. button, string, and a hot glue gun

HOMESPUN ANGEL

1. Steep tea in two cups of boiling water and allow to cool. Soak doilies in tea until desired shade is achieved; allow to dry. Press doilies.

2. For dress, tear a $12^{1}/2$" x 17" rectangle from muslin. Spacing 4" apart, glue $5/8$" dia. buttons along one long edge of dress. Use pen to write message between buttons.

(Continued on page 148)

SNOWMAN LUMINARIES

These adorable ornaments will receive glowing remarks when you hang them on the evergreen! Illuminated by miniature Christmas lights, the chilly weather guys are created from sponge-painted jars. A ladies' knit glove provides a cuddly hat for each ornament.

WHAT TO BUY

Package of bamboo skewers and a pair of ladies' knit gloves

THINGS YOU HAVE AT HOME

Two small jars with lids; large nail; hammer; natural sponge; white, orange, and black acrylic paint; small stencil brush; small paintbrush; needle; thread; green yarn; clear nylon thread; scrap of plaid fabric; four white buttons; dried greenery; and a hot glue gun

LUMINOUS SNOWMAN ORNAMENTS

Allow paint to dry after each application.

1. For each ornament, remove lid from jar. Use hammer and nail to make a hole in center of lid large enough for miniature Christmas light. Replace lid on jar.

2. Follow *Painting Basics*, page 188, and use white paint to sponge paint outside of jar. Use stencil brush to paint snowman eyes and mouth black. For nose, cut a 1" length from one end of skewer; paint orange. Glue nose to jar. Paint glue white.

3. For hat, cut fingers and thumb from one glove. Leaving thumb opening for

inserting light, hand baste around top of glove; pull threads to gather. Tie thread ends and clip. Referring to *Making a Pom-pom,* page 191, use yarn to make a pom-pom. Sew pom-pom to gathers of hat.

4. For hanger, thread ends of a 10" length of nylon thread through pom-pom and top of hat; knot ends together. Roll up cuff of hat. Positioning light opening at back of ornament, glue hat around top of jar.

5. For scarf, tear a ³/₄" x 14" strip of fabric; tie strip around bottom of jar. Glue buttons to scarf and hat. Glue greenery to hat.

6. To light ornament, hang on tree and insert miniature bulb from Christmas lights through holes in hat and jar.

PAINTBRUSH PALS

Whimsical felt faces add pleasing personality to our clever Santa ornaments. You can make three of these jolly paintbrush pals for next to nothing. They make great offerings for friends and neighbors!

WHAT TO BUY

Three $2^1/_2$" x $8^1/_2$" paintbrushes; one white, one ecru, one pink, one black, and two red felt pieces; black embroidery floss; $^1/_8$ yd. of artificial lamb's wool; and three 1" dia. pom-poms

THINGS YOU HAVE AT HOME

Tracing paper, pinking shears, white acrylic paint, small paintbrush, thread, and a hot glue gun

PAINTBRUSH SANTAS

1. Trace patterns, page 157, onto tracing paper. For each Santa, use patterns to cut eyes from white felt, irises from black felt, and cheeks, nose, and chin from pink felt. Use pinking shears to cut head shape from ecru felt. Arrange face pieces on head; glue in place.

2. For highlights, apply a dot of white paint on each eye and nose.

(Continued on page 148)

COUNTRY ANGELS

*S*pread glad tidings with these charming country angels. There's no sewing involved, and it's a heavenly way to "recycle" brown paper bags! These ornaments are also great treats for co-workers.

WHAT TO BUY

1/8 yd. of fabric and 1/3 yd. of 1/8"w ribbon

THINGS YOU HAVE AT HOME

Paper-backed fusible web, scraps of assorted fabric, brown paper bag, black permanent felt-tip pen, pink colored pencil, facial tissues, natural raffia, scraps of red embroidery floss, wire cutters, craft wire, clear nylon thread, and craft glue

PAPER BAG ANGEL ORNAMENTS

1. Follow *Fusing Basics*, page 187, and use patterns, page 160, to make angel A, angel B, and two 1" square patch appliqués from fabric and fabric scraps.

2. For each ornament, cut two 6" x 9" rectangles from paper bag. Arrange appliqués on one rectangle; fuse in place. Cut 1/4" outside edge of appliqués.

3. Use pen to draw "stitches" around collar, patch, and border of ornament and to draw eyes and mouth. Use pink pencil to color cheeks.

4. For back of each ornament, draw around ornament front on remaining paper rectangle; cut out. Leaving an opening for stuffing, glue front and back ornament edges together. Stuff ornament lightly with tissues; glue opening closed.

5. For hair, cut several 4" lengths of raffia; knot ends together with embroidery floss; glue hair to angel's head. Cut a 3" length of embroidery floss; tie into a bow. Glue bow to collar.

6. For halo, cut a 5" length of craft wire and bend into an oval shape; twist ends together and glue above hair.

7. For hanger, fold a 6" length of thread in half and knot ends together; glue to back of ornament.

STELLAR ORNAMENTS

*N*ow there's a way to display all your holiday "stars" on the Christmas tree! In just a little time, you can make a galaxy of stellar photo ornaments featuring all your favorite faces.

WHAT TO BUY
Five 3³/₄"w plastic star ornaments, gold spray paint, ¹/₈ yd. of Christmas print fabric, and ¹/₈"w red satin ribbon (10-yd. spool)

THINGS YOU HAVE AT HOME
Poster board, paper-backed fusible web, photographs, ¹/₈" dia. hole punch, and craft glue

STAR PHOTO ORNAMENTS
1. Paint each ornament; allow to dry.

2. Cut two 4¹/₄" x 24" rectangles each from fabric and fusible web and one from poster board. Follow web manufacturer's instructions to fuse fabric to both sides of poster board. Draw around star ornament five times on fabric-covered poster board. Cut out each shape just inside drawn line.

3. Draw around fused star shape on desired photographs; cut out ¹/₄" inside drawn line. Center photograph on one side of fabric star and glue in place. Punch a hole in top point of star.

4. Cut five 8" and five 15" lengths of ribbon. For each ornament hanger, thread one 15" ribbon through hole in star and ornament; knot close to ornament. Knot ends of streamers together. Tie one 8" ribbon into a bow around each hanger.

JOLLY OLD ELF

*L*et St. Nick's jolly mug brighten your tree! The padded ornament is easy to make from felt and embellish with a raffia beard. Craft a pair — you can keep them both for yourself or share with a friend.

WHAT TO BUY

Ecru felt piece, brown embroidery floss, $1/4$" dia. jingle bell, $1/16$"w green ribbon (10-yd. spool), and natural raffia

THINGS YOU HAVE AT HOME

Tracing paper, scraps of pink and red fabrics, drawing compass, pinking shears, polyester fiberfill, and a hot glue gun

SANTA FACE ORNAMENTS

Refer to Embroidery Stitches, page 189, before beginning project. Use six strands of floss for all stitching.

1. Trace patterns, page 162, onto tracing paper. For each ornament, use patterns to cut one nose and two cheeks from pink fabric. Fold cheek pattern in half; use to cut one mouth from red fabric.

2. For head/hat pattern, use compass to draw a $4^1/4$" dia. circle on tracing paper. Use pattern and pinking shears to cut two heads from felt and one hat from red fabric.

3. Using embroidery floss, work long Straight Stitches to sew cheeks and nose on one head shape. Work French Knots for eyes. Glue mouth on face.

4. Matching wrong sides and leaving an opening for stuffing, use floss to whipstitch head pieces together. Stuff with fiberfill; sew opening closed.

5. For hat, fold red $4^1/2$" circle in half. Insert 1" of head between layers at fold; glue in place. For point, fold remainder of hat to front; glue in place. Tie a 4" length of ribbon into a bow; glue bow and a jingle bell to point of hat.

6. For beard and mustache, cut several 8" lengths of raffia. Place lengths together and knot in center. Repeat to make six bundles. Glue one bundle under nose for mustache, and five bundles along bottom of mouth for beard.

7. For hanger, cut a 6" length of clear nylon thread; knot ends and sew to back of ornament.

FOLK-ART MITTENS

*A*dd a toasty touch to the evergreen with cozy corduroy mittens. These folksy ornaments are appliquéd with felt flowers and trimmed in blanket stitching for a country look. Make a handful of them!

WHAT TO BUY

$1/2$ yd. each of red corduroy and heavy-weight fusible interfacing; one gold, one green, and three white felt pieces; green embroidery floss; and $3/8$"w red satin ribbon (10-yd. spool)

THINGS YOU HAVE AT HOME

Tracing paper, paper-backed fusible web, embroidery needle, pinking shears, buttons, and craft glue

MITTEN ORNAMENTS

1. Follow manufacturer's instructions to fuse interfacing to wrong side of corduroy.

2. Trace pattern, page 153, onto tracing paper. Using pattern, cut two mitten shapes (one in reverse) for each ornament from corduroy.

3. Referring to *Fusing Basics,* page 187, use patterns, page 153, to make flower and flower center appliqués from felt. Fuse flower center appliqué on flower.

4. Using three strands of floss, work Blanket Stitch, page 189, around edge of flower. Arrange appliqués on right side of one mitten shape; fuse in place. Sew a button to flower center.

5. Matching wrong sides, place mitten front and back together; pin in place. Use Blanket Stitch to sew mitten pieces together, leaving top edge open.

6. For cuff, use pinking shears to cut a 3" x 7" rectangle from white felt.

Overlapping short ends at back, glue cuff to top of mitten; allow to dry. Fold cuff over top of mitten.

7. For hanger, cut a 6" length of ribbon. Fold ribbon in half and sew ends to inside top edge of cuff.

ELFIN MAGIC

Add a little elfin magic to the season with this whimsical ornament! He's fashioned from print fabrics and felt pieces, and a chenille twist candy cane serves as a cute hanger.

WHAT TO BUY

Flesh, red, green, and black felt pieces; red and white striped chenille twists; $1/4$" dia. red pom-poms; and a 6mm jingle bell

THINGS YOU HAVE AT HOME

Tracing paper, scraps of Christmas print fabrics, utility scissors, jute twine, scrap of black embroidery floss, and a hot glue gun

ELF ORNAMENT

1. Trace patterns, page 161, onto tracing paper; cut out. Using patterns, cut one hat, one collar, two heads, four hands, and two feet from felt pieces and two shirts from fabric.

2. For arms, cut two $3/4$" x 12" strips of fabric. Center a chenille twist along wrong side of one arm strip; glue in place. Matching wrong sides and long edges, glue arm strips together; use utility scissors to cut in half. Glue one end of each arm between two hands. Glue remaining ends at an angle between shoulders on wrong side of shirt back.

3. For legs, cut two $1/2$" x 6" strips of fabric. Matching wrong sides, glue legs together; cut in half. Glue one end of each leg to wrong side of shirt back along bottom edge; glue feet to remaining ends of legs. Matching wrong sides, glue shirt front to shirt back.

4. Glue head shapes together. For hair, cut a 2" length of twine; untwist slightly. Glue hair and hat on head. Fold top of hat over and glue in place. Glue head and collar to shirt.

5. Bend arms to make "elbows" and make hands meet over elf's head. Cut a 6" length from chenille twist; bend into a candy cane shape. Glue candy cane between hands.

6. Glue one pom-pom to each toe and one to face for nose. For mouth, cut a $1^1/2$" length of floss; glue one strand to face. Glue jingle bell to tip of hat.

*B*ring a touch of nostalgia to the tree with this charming heart, or select brighter shades of felt for a modern look. The pockets would also make nice little gifts or party favors — just fill them with peppermint sticks or other treats.

WHAT TO BUY
Ecru, red, green, and dark green felt pieces

THINGS YOU HAVE AT HOME
Pinking shears, paper-backed fusible web, black embroidery floss, and six assorted small and large white buttons

HEART POCKET ORNAMENT
Refer to Embroidery Stitches, page 189, before beginning project. Use three strands of floss for all stitching.

1. For hanger, use pinking shears to cut a $1/2$" x $8^1/2$" strip from dark green felt piece; set aside. Matching short edges, fold and cut all felt pieces in half.

2. Follow *Fusing Basics,* page 187, and use patterns, page 166, to make heart and leaf appliqués. For each side of ornament, use pinking shears to cut small heart appliqué from red felt. Cut large heart appliqué from dark green felt. Center red heart on green heart; fuse in place. Position fused hearts on one ecru felt piece; fuse in place. Use pinking shears to cut out ecru heart $1/8$" from edge of green heart.

3. Sew ends of hanger to wrong sides of hearts as indicated in Fig. 1.

Fig. 1

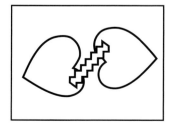

4. For flower, stack one small button on larger button; use floss to sew in place on red heart. Arrange leaf appliqués near flower; fuse in place.

5. Covering hanger stitching, sew remaining buttons onto front and back of ornament.

6. Matching wrong sides and leaving top edges of pocket open, work Running Stitch around edges to sew hearts together.

SUPER SNOWFLAKES

*H*ere's a super project idea to share with a friend — adorable snowflake snowmen ornaments. You can make two for just a few dollars, so keep one for yourself and give the other to a favorite pal!

WHAT TO BUY

2" dia. plastic foam ball, textured snow medium, 5mm black flat-back beads, black craft foam, 1/3 yd. of 7/8"w plaid ribbon, and two 5" dia. acrylic snowflake ornaments

THINGS YOU HAVE AT HOME

Serrated knife, plastic sandwich bag, paintbrush, white and orange acrylic paint, tracing paper, drawing compass, cardboard tube from paper towels, and a hot glue gun

SNOWFLAKE SNOWMEN

1. Use knife to cut foam ball in half. Follow manufacturer's instructions to apply snow to rounded side of each half; allow to dry.

2. For nose, place a small amount of snow medium in corner of plastic bag. Cut tip from corner of bag. Squeeze nose shape onto each snowman face; allow to dry. Paint noses orange.

3. Glue five beads to each face for mouth. Trace pattern, page 154, onto tracing paper. Using pattern, cut four eyes from craft foam. Paint a white dot in each eye. Glue eyes to each face.

4. For hats, use compass to draw a 2 1/2" dia. circle on craft foam; cut out. Cut a 1" long section from cardboard tube. Position tube section cut side down at center of foam circle; draw around outside. Cut foam circle and tube piece in half. Cut inner half-circle from each foam circle half. Measure tube piece; cut two pieces of craft foam the determined measurement. Glue foam pieces to outside of each tube piece. Glue each hat brim and tube piece together. Glue one inner half-circle to top of each hat.

5. Glue one snowman head to center of each snowflake.

6. For scarves, cut ribbon in half; tie a knot in center of each half. Glue one scarf to bottom of each snowman head.

ONE-HOUR TREE TRIMMING

Make this the year to add pizzazz to your tree with clever, quickly assembled tree-trimmers. Sprinkle your evergreen with fast-to-fix projects such as Santas, stars, and snowmen to create an air of elegance, rustic charm, or playfulness. You'll find shiny glass ornaments accented with unique designs and a precious photo surrounded by a golden circle of buttons. You can also whip up a cinnamon-stick angel or a whimsical snowman crafted from a washcloth. Our delightful baubles are sure to make holiday spirits soar!

*W*ith a wave of his wand, this jolly old elf will bring holiday magic to your Christmas tree! Our primitive Santa is simple to make using padded fabric-covered bristol board and painted craft sticks. He's sure to make the holidays special.

MAGIC SANTA ORNAMENT

You will need: tracing paper; drawing compass; $4^1/2$" squares of bristol board and batting; $5/8$" dia. button; $4^1/2$" length of $3/8$"w black grosgrain ribbon; paintbrush; black paint; jumbo craft stick; scraps of two red fabrics, white felt, and red felt; white thread; $3/8$" dia. button; 3"w wooden heart cutout; black pen; red colored pencil; $1^1/2$"w wooden star cutout; wooden craft pick; and a hot glue gun and glue sticks.

1. For Santa body, use tracing paper and compass to make $3^1/2$" dia. and $4^1/2$" dia. circle patterns. Use $3^1/2$" pattern to cut one circle each from bristol board and batting. Glue batting circle to bristol board circle.

2. Use $4^1/2$" pattern to cut circle from one red fabric. Center glued circles batting side down on wrong side of fabric circle. Wrap fabric edges to back of circle; glue in place.

3. For belt and buckle, sew larger button to center of ribbon. Center and glue ribbon to body, wrapping ends to back.

4. Use $3^1/2$" pattern to cut one circle from red felt; glue over back of body.

5. For arms, paint ends of craft stick black; allow to dry. For sleeves, cut a 2" x 4" rectangle from remaining red fabric; center and glue around craft stick. For cuffs, cut two $1/2$" x $2^1/4$" strips of white felt; glue one strip around craft stick at end of each sleeve.

6. Trace beard and hat patterns (pg. 182) onto tracing paper. Use patterns to cut hat from red felt and beard from white felt.

7. With heart cutout upside down, wrap hat around point, overlapping at back; glue in place. For hatband, cut a $1/4$" x 3" strip of white felt; glue to bottom of hat, overlapping ends at back. Sew small button to top of hat.

8. Use pen to draw eyes and red pencil to color cheeks. Glue beard just below center of cheeks.

9. Center head on arms; glue in place. Center arms on top front of body; glue in place. Glue wooden star to craft pick; glue craft pick to hand.

*C*reate *a galaxy of heavenly ornaments using painted wooden stars! Corrugated cardboard accented with colorful buttons adds a textured touch to the bright pieces.*

WOODEN STAR ORNAMENTS

For each ornament, you will need:
5" wooden star, acrylic paint, paintbrush, corrugated craft cardboard, gold craft wire, pencil, assorted buttons, and glue.

1. Paint star desired color; allow to dry.

2. Draw around wooden star on cardboard. Cut out cardboard star $1/4$" inside drawn line. Center cardboard star, corrugated side up, on wooden star; glue in place.

3. Cut a 15" length of craft wire. Wrap 3" of each end of wire around pencil to curl.

4. Thread each end of wire through a button; twist at back of button to secure. Bend wire into an arc and glue to back of star.

5. Glue assorted buttons to front of ornament.

GOOD-AS-GOLD ORNAMENT

IN ONLY 8 MINUTES!

This glimmering bauble is as good as gold! And it's so quick to make, you can craft one for everyone you know. Simply wrap a matte-finish ornament with shiny trim, top it with a silk poinsettia, and attach a gold cord hanger.

LUSTROUS GOLD ORNAMENT

You will need: gold silk poinsettia, 3½" dia. gold matte-finish ornament, 10" length of ⅝"w gold trim, 8" length of gold cord, and a hot glue gun and glue sticks.

1. Remove petals, leaves, and flower center from poinsettia.

2. Glue leaves, then petals around top of ornament.

3. Glue trim around center of ornament.

4. Thread flower center through ornament hanger and glue in place.

5. Thread cord through hanger; knot ends together.

T his stunning tree topper will capture the attention of star-gazers! Gilded trim outlines the shimmering brocade patchwork, and a golden cord bow provides an elegant finish.

BROCADE STAR TREE TOPPER

You will need: tracing paper, poster board, paper-backed fusible web, scraps of five assorted brocade lamé fabrics, 1¹/₃ yds. of ³/₈"w gold trim, 36" long gold cord with tasseled ends, 3" length of floral wire, and a hot glue gun and glue sticks.

1. Referring to *Making Patterns* (pg. 187), trace star pattern (pg. 181) onto tracing paper; cut out. Use pattern to cut one star from poster board.

2. Referring to *Fusing Basics* (pg. 187), use pattern to make five star segment appliqués from fabrics. Arrange appliqués on poster board star; fuse in place.

3. Glue gold trim around all edges of appliqués.

4. Tie cord into a double bow; glue bow to center of star.

5. For hanger, bend floral wire to form a loop; glue loop to back of star.

HOMESPUN TREE-TRIMMER

*N*eed some quick and easy tree-trimmers to share with co-workers or neighbors? This homespun ornament is the perfect project! Just wrap fabric around a plastic foam ball, gather with ribbon, and add a starry accent.

FABRIC-COVERED ORNAMENT

You will need: paintbrush, yellow acrylic paint, two 4"w wooden star cutouts, black pen, drawing compass, newspaper, 12" square of fabric, 3" dia. foam ball, rubber band, 1 yd. of ¼"w green ribbon, floral pin, and a hot glue gun and glue sticks.

1. Apply one coat of paint to each star; allow to dry.

2. Use compass to make a 12" circle pattern from newspaper. Use pattern to cut one shape from fabric square.

3. Center foam ball on wrong side of fabric circle. Gather edges of fabric around foam ball. Wrap rubber band around gathers to secure; adjust gathers.

4. Cut an 18" length of ribbon; tie into a bow around gathers, covering rubber band.

5. Cut a 14" length of ribbon; fold in half. Matching star edges, glue folded ribbon between stars, leaving a 2" loop at top for hanger. Use pen to draw "stitches" around edges of each star.

6. Tie remaining ends of ribbon into a knot. Insert floral pen through knot and into top of ornament.

IN ONLY
20
MINUTES!

With her cute button face, this little angel is sure to bring a country air to your tree! Her simple attire is made of felt and buttons, and her freckled face is easy to draw using markers. Yarn doll hair crowns her with curls, and chenille stem "wings" are ready to take flight.

FRECKLED ANGEL ORNAMENT

You will need: $3^1/_2$" x 4" pieces of poster board, ecru felt, and paper-backed fusible web; tracing paper; scraps of gold felt and muslin; $1^1/_8$" dia. covered button kit; brown and black markers; brown curly yarn doll hair; two brown chenille stems; 6" length of gold craft wire; six assorted brown buttons; 4" length of floral wire; gold embroidery floss; and a hot glue gun and glue sticks.

1. Following manufacturer's instructions, use web to fuse felt to poster board.

2. Trace small angel body and star patterns (pg. 179) onto tracing paper; cut out. Use pattern to cut angel from fused rectangle.

3. Use pattern to cut one star from gold felt; glue to felt side of angel body.

4. For angel head, follow manufacturer's instructions to cover button with muslin. Use markers to draw face and freckles.

5. Cut a small amount of curly yarn and glue to top of head. Glue head to angel body.

6. For wings, cut two 8" lengths of chenille stems. Bend stems into wing shapes; glue to back of ornament.

7. For halo, bend craft wire into a circle; twist ends together. Glue halo to back of head.

8. Glue buttons to front of ornament.

9. For hanger, bend floral wire into a hook; glue to back of ornament.

10. Cut two 12" lengths of embroidery floss. Place lengths together; tie into a bow. Glue bow to angel under chin.

JOLLY SANTA BELL

*R*ing in the holidays with an ornament fashioned after everyone's favorite gift-giver! Transfer paper makes it a cinch to paint Santa's jolly face onto a papier-mâché bell. A fluffy pom-pom tops his hat.

SANTA BELL ORNAMENT

You will need: white, flesh, cream, pink, red, very light grey, and black acrylic paint; paintbrushes; tracing paper; transfer paper; stylus; 4"h papier-mâché bell ornament; black pen; 20mm pom-pom; and craft glue.

1. Paint ornament white; allow to dry.

2. Trace Santa face pattern (pg. 180) onto tracing paper. Use stylus and transfer paper to transfer pattern to bell. Extend hat and hat trim lines around back of ornament.

3. Using transferred lines as a guide, paint face flesh and cap and mouth red. Using a stamping motion, paint hat trim cream. Use pink paint to paint nose, cheek lines, and lips. Use very light grey paint to shade area below mustache. Allow to dry.

4. Use black pen to draw eyes and to add detail lines. Use white paint to highlight eyes, nose, and cheeks; paint eyebrows; and paint dots on hat.

5. Glue pom-pom to top of ornament; allow to dry.

*M*aking this cheery ornament is child's play! Wooden alphabet blocks and beads are laced onto craft wire, which is shaped into a ring. Berry sprigs and a wooden star give the hanger festive charm.

CIRCLE OF JOY ORNAMENT

You will need: craft drill, wooden alphabet blocks to spell JOY, wire cutters, black craft wire, red and green wooden beads, pencil, holly berry sprigs, 2"w wooden star, and a hot glue gun and glue sticks.

1. Use craft drill to drill a hole horizontally through center of each block.

2. Use wire cutters to cut a 28" length of craft wire. Thread wire through one red and one green bead, through Y block, through one green bead, through O block, through one green bead, through J block, and through one green and one red bead.

3. Bend wire into a circle. Cross wires 5" from ends; twist wires together at top of circle. Wrap wire ends around pencil to curl.

4. Cut a 12" length of wire; bend to form hanging loop. Attach loop to top of circle by twisting wires together at bottom of loop; curl ends.

5. Wrap ends of berry sprigs around base of loop; glue in place. Glue blocks in place on wire.

6. Glue wooden star over base of hanging loop.

A "snowcapped" pinecone makes a perfect perch for this vibrant feathered friend! A sprig of wintertime berries finishes the ornament with Yuletide spirit — in only seven minutes!

CARDINAL ORNAMENT

You will need: textured snow medium, large pinecone, 12" length of ¹/₈"w red ribbon, artificial cardinal, and craft glue.

1. For hanger, fold ribbon in half, forming a loop. Tie a knot 2" from fold; glue ribbon ends under one wing of bird.

2. Follow manufacturer's instructions to apply snow medium to top of pinecone, leaving a 1" dia. opening at center top of pinecone.

3. Glue bird onto snow, covering opening. Allow to dry.

*S*hare a touch of country charm with these rustic rag ball ornaments. They're super-fast to create using strips of torn fabric wrapped over foam balls. Buttons from your stash top off the natural raffia bows.

RAG BALL ORNAMENTS

For each ornament, you will need:
3" dia. foam ball, ¹/₈ yd. of fabric, natural raffia, button, and a hot glue gun and glue sticks.

1. Tear seven 1¹/₄" x 9" strips of fabric; press.

2. Overlapping long edges and twisting fabric at bottom of ball, wrap six fabric strips around ball. Glue ends of strips in place at top of ball; allow to dry.

3. For ornament hanger, glue ends of remaining fabric strip together, forming a loop. Glue to top of ornament.

4. Cut several 4" lengths of raffia; use one length of raffia to tie remaining lengths together at center. Glue to hanger.

5. Glue button over raffia.

GILDED BAUBLES

Here's a great way to dress up ordinary glass baubles. Simply spray assorted trims with adhesive and apply them to the ornaments as you please. Your creativity is what makes these accents unique!

ELEGANT ORNAMENTS

For each ornament, you will need: assorted gold, silver, and ecru trims; newspaper; spray adhesive; 3" dia. gold glass ornament; and a 7" length of gold cord.

1. Cut trims into 9$\frac{1}{2}$" lengths.

2. Place trims on newspaper wrong side up; spray with adhesive.

3. Wrap trims around ornament as desired, trimming ends as necessary.

4. Thread cord through hanger; knot ends together.

*B*rilliant baubles of gold lamé adorn this easy-to-decorate skirt. Any plain purchased tree skirt can be used as a base for the gilded motifs. No-sew fusing makes them simple to attach. Glue on touches of ribbon and braid for extra special embellishments.

ELEGANT TREE SKIRT

You will need: ecru tree skirt, paper-backed fusible web, $^1/_4$ yd. of gold lamé fabric, 1"w fusible web tape, aluminum foil, $1^1/_4$"w gold trim, $^3/_8$"w gold trim, and $1^1/_2$ yds. of $^5/_8$"w gold mesh ribbon.

1. Referring to *Fusing Basics* (pg. 187), use patterns (pgs. 183) to make one ornament B and two ornament A appliqués from gold lamé.

2. Arrange appliqués on tree skirt and fuse in place.

3. Referring to *Fusing Basics* (pg. 187), follow Foil Method to fuse web tape to

wrong side of $1^1/_4$"w gold trim. Cut trim into lengths to fit across ornaments. Arrange trim on ornaments and fuse in place.

4. Measure distances from inner edge of tree skirt to top of each ornament; cut a length of $^3/_8$"w trim for each of the determined measurements. Fuse web tape to wrong side of trims; arrange on tree skirt and fuse in place.

5. Cut three 18" lengths of gold mesh ribbon. Tie each length into a bow and glue one bow to top of each ornament.

CUPFUL OF LOVE

*O*ur little Santa bear looks so sweet nestled in a decorated teacup! The tiny packages that fill his arms are crafted by wrapping plastic foam pieces with scraps of festive felt.

TEACUP BEAR

You will need: tracing paper; scraps of white, red, and green felt; 10mm white pom-pom; two small rectangles of plastic foam; 18" length of $1/8$"w red ribbon; 6" length of $1/8$"w green ribbon; white teacup; red and green paint pens; 6" tall stuffed bear, 8" length of heavy gauge floral wire; and a hot glue gun and glue sticks.

1. Trace bear hat and bear hat trim patterns (pg. 170) onto tracing paper; cut out. Use patterns to cut one hat from red felt and one hat trim from white felt. Overlap short edges of hat and glue in place, trimming as necessary. Glue hat trim around bottom of hat. Scrunch hat down on bear's head; glue in place. Glue pom-pom to point of hat.

2. For packages, wrap each foam piece with red or green felt; glue in place. Glue a ribbon length around each package.

3. Use red pen to draw ribbons and stripes on cup. Use green pen to draw dots on cup.

4. Glue bear inside cup.

5. For hanger, twist one end of floral wire around bear's neck; bend remaining end of wire into a loop.

6. Tie remaining red ribbon into a bow around bear's neck, covering wire.

*W*hat better place for Santa than atop the tree! Our muslin fellow adds a cute country touch to the evergreen. His clothes are made using simple patterns, and his face is easy to apply with marking pens.

SANTA TREE TOPPER

You will need: 17"h muslin doll, black fabric paint, paintbrush, wood-tone spray, small muslin drawstring bag, tracing paper, ³⁄₈ yd. of red fabric, natural and bleached wool roving, tan and brown markers, 30" length of jute twine, polyester fiberfill, small sprig of artificial greenery, and a hot glue gun and glue sticks.

1. Paint doll's hands and feet black. Lightly spray drawstring bag with wood-tone spray; allow to dry.

2. Referring to *Making Patterns* (pg. 187), trace Santa coat pattern (pg. 177) onto tracing paper. Cut a 12" x 16" piece of fabric. Matching right sides and short edges, fold fabric in half. Aligning shoulders of pattern with fold of fabric, use pattern to cut out Santa coat.

3. Using a ¹⁄₄" seam allowance, stitch underarm and side seams; turn right side out and press. For coat trim, cut one 16" and two 10" lengths of bleached roving; glue 16" length around bottom of coat and one 10" length around each cuff.

4. For pants, cut two 5¹⁄₄" x 10" rectangles from fabric. Place rectangles right sides together. Referring to Fig. 1, stitch side and inner leg seams. Cut up to but not through inside of inner leg seams. Turn right side out and press. For pants trim, cut two 6" lengths of bleached roving; glue one length around bottom of each pants leg.

Fig. 1

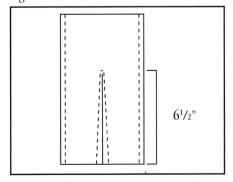

5. For hood, cut a 5" x 8" rectangle from fabric. Baste along three edges, leaving one 8" edge unstitched. Gather basting slightly. For hood trim, cut an 8" length of bleached roving; glue along straight edge of hood.

6. Use markers to draw face on doll. For beard, cut a 4" length of natural roving. Stitch across one end of beard to hold in place. Glue beard to doll face.

7. Place clothing on doll, gluing in place where necessary. Tie twine around waist over coat.

8. Stuff drawstring bag with a small amount of fiberfill; place bag on Santa's arm.

9. Glue greenery sprig to one hand.

A personalized ornament is a great way to share holiday cheer with your favorite families! Our hand-painted glass bauble is simple to decorate — a felt-tip pen makes it easy to apply the name and "stitches."

PERSONALIZED ORNAMENT

You will need: tracing paper, 3¹/₂" dia. frosted glass ornament, pencil, paintbrush, red and green enamel glass paint, and a black felt-tip pen.

1. Trace star pattern (pg. 171) onto tracing paper; cut out. Carefully cut along lines at center of pattern.

2. Remove hanger from ornament. Place center cuts of pattern over ornament opening and press pattern to ornament. Use pencil to trace around pattern; remove pattern.

3. Center pattern at bottom of ornament and trace around pattern.

4. Paint stars red. Use end of paintbrush to apply dots of green paint at each point of stars. Allow paint to dry.

5. Use pen to draw "stitches" around stars and to write name on ornament.

6. Replace ornament hanger.

This heavenly tree-trimmer smells as good as it looks! Our darling cinnamon angel will dress any evergreen in warm country charm. Easy to create from cinnamon sticks and a foam tube, she'll be a spicy addition to your Christmas decorating.

CINNAMON ANGEL

You will need: serrated knife, 1" dia. foam tube, 2$\frac{1}{2}$" x 4" piece of muslin, $\frac{2}{3}$ yd. of 2$\frac{1}{2}$"w wired ribbon for dress, 4" length of $\frac{1}{4}$"w flat lace, two 6" long cinnamon sticks, $\frac{1}{2}$ yd. of 2$\frac{1}{2}$"w mesh wired ribbon for wings, 3" length of floral wire, miniature pinecones, artificial greenery, black pen, red colored pencil, 12" length of $\frac{1}{4}$"w red satin ribbon, 8" length of clear nylon thread, and a hot glue gun and glue sticks.

1. For doll body, use serrated knife to cut a 4$\frac{1}{2}$" length of foam tube, tapering one end for head.

2. With fabric extending $\frac{1}{2}$" beyond head end of foam tube, wrap muslin around tube; glue in place. Fold excess fabric over and glue in place.

3. Cut the following pieces from ribbon for dress: one 10" length for skirt, one 4" length for bodice, and two 2$\frac{1}{2}$" lengths for sleeves.

4. Overlapping ends at back, wrap bodice around foam tube; glue in place. For collar, glue flat lace around top of bodice.

5. Holding wire end of one edge of ribbon for skirt, gather ribbon. Adjusting gathers to fit around doll body, twist wires together to secure over bottom of bodice; glue in place.

6. For arms, cut one cinnamon stick in half. Gather ribbon for sleeves. Wrap one sleeve around each arm; glue in place. Glue arms to doll.

7. For legs, insert remaining cinnamon stick into bottom of doll body; glue in place.

8. For wings, bring ends of mesh ribbon to center of ribbon, overlapping $\frac{1}{2}$". Pinch together and secure with floral wire. Glue wings to back of doll at shoulders.

9. For hair, glue pinecones to doll head. Glue sprig of greenery in hair.

10. Use pen to draw face on doll; use red pencil to color cheeks.

11. Tie satin ribbon into a bow around waist of doll.

12. For hanger, fold nylon thread in half; knot to form a loop. Glue knot to back of ornament.

*L*et a snowy friend decorate your tree in frosty style! A papier-mâché bell is painted and dressed with "buttons" and a fabric scrap "scarf" to create the character. He's a snap to complete in just 10 minutes!

SNOWMAN BELL ORNAMENT
You will need: white, orange, and black acrylic paint; $2^1/2$"h papier-mâché bell ornament; three black beads; $^1/_2$" x 9" torn fabric strip; small nail; two small twigs; and a hot glue gun and glue sticks.

1. Paint ornament white; allow to dry.

2. Paint an orange dot for nose and black dots for eyes and mouth.

3. For buttons, glue beads to front of snowman.

4. For scarf, tie fabric strip around ornament and glue in place.

5. For arms, use nail to punch a hole in each side of ornament. Glue end of one twig into each hole.

Our wooden spoon angel spreads holiday cheer and whimsical charm from her lofty perch atop the tree. Dressed up with assorted buttons and flyaway twig hair, the quick-to-complete angel can also shine as a package decoration.

BUTTON ANGEL

You will need: antique white acrylic paint; paintbrush; wooden spoon; two jumbo craft sticks; two 4¼" long wooden heart cutouts; 10" squares of foam core board, ecru fabric, and paper-backed fusible web; tracing paper; craft knife; black felt-tip marker; pink colored pencil; small twigs; 1½" dia. white shank button; 9" length of 1½"w flat ecru lace; assorted buttons; 6" length of floral wire; and a hot glue gun and glue sticks.

1. Apply one coat of white paint to one side of wooden spoon, craft sticks, and heart cutouts; allow to dry.

2. Referring to *Fusing Basics* (pg. 187), use web to fuse wrong side of fabric to foam core board.

3. Trace large angel body pattern (pg. 178) onto tracing paper; cut out. Draw around pattern on fused foam core board; use craft knife to cut out shape.

4. Use marker to draw eyes and mouth on spoon for doll face and to draw shoes on craft sticks. Use pink pencil to color cheeks.

5. For hair, glue several twigs to top of spoon. For halo, glue white shank button to top back of spoon.

6. Glue lace 1" from bottom of body, wrapping ends to back. Glue buttons to body; glue one small button over each shoe.

7. Glue spoon handle, tips of hearts (wings), and 2½" of each craft stick (legs) to back of body.

8. For hanger, fold floral wire in half to form a loop; twist ends together. Glue to back of spoon near tips of wings.

IN ONLY
25
MINUTES!

When you need to cook up a batch of unique tree-trimmers in a jiffy, these antique-look ornaments are made to order! The aged patina of the cookie cutters is created using a simple painting technique. For a bit of rustic elegance, finish them with raffia bows.

AGED COOKIE CUTTERS
You will need: black acrylic paint; sponge paintbrush; angel, star, and heart metal cookie cutters; weathering paint for metal; and natural raffia.

1. Thin black paint with a small amount of water. Use sponge brush to apply a thin coat of black paint to each cookie cutter; allow to dry slightly.

2. Apply one coat of weathering paint over black paint; allow to dry.

3. Cut several 12" lengths of raffia. Tie lengths into a knot around each cookie cutter. Trim ends.

*W*hat a handsome fellow! This friendly, fuzzy reindeer will be a happy addition to the Christmas tree. He's crafted from shaggy felt, and his features are made with felt scraps. Jingle bells wrapped around each antler give our red-nosed friend a merry touch.

REINDEER ORNAMENT

You will need: tracing paper; poster board; fabric marking pencil; batting scraps; brown shaggy felt; scraps of white, red, and black felt; white embroidery floss; small twigs for antlers; wired stem with jingle bells; and a hot glue gun and glue sticks.

1. Trace reindeer upper head, lower head, ear, eye, and nose patterns (pg. 171) onto tracing paper; cut out.

2. Use upper and lower head patterns to cut shapes from poster board and batting. Glue batting to poster board shapes.

3. Cutting $1/2$" outside upper and lower head patterns, cut one of each shape from brown felt. Cut two ears from brown felt.

4. Center and glue felt head shapes over batting side of poster board shapes, wrapping excess to back. Position $1^1/2$" of right side of upper head behind wrong side of lower head; glue in place.

5. Fold ears in half lengthwise. Glue square end of each together; glue to top back of head.

6. Use eye pattern to cut two shapes each from white and black felt. Use nose pattern to cut shape from red felt.

7. Use six strands of white floss to stitch details in black eyes and nose.

8. Glue nose to reindeer lower head; glue white, then black eyes to upper head, overlapping so that small amount of white eyes show.

9. For mouth, cut a $1/4$" x 3" strip and two $1/4$" x $1/2$" strips from black felt. Glue strips in place.

10. For antlers, wrap a length of jingle bell stem around each twig. Glue twigs to back of head.

11. For ornament hanger, cut a 3" length of floral wire; bend to form a loop and glue to top back of head.

12. Use upper and lower head patterns to cut one shape of each from brown felt. Glue upper head, then lower head to back of reindeer.

13. For scarf, cut a $3/4$" x 12" length of red felt; fringe ends. Tie into a loose knot and glue under reindeer's chin.

COLORFUL FELT CANDLE

With their warm, mood-setting glow, candles are lovely, nostalgic complements to seasonal merriment. Our three-dimensional candle is fashioned from felt and finished with a wooden star and buttons. You can complete one of these heartwarming ornaments in a mere 15 minutes!

FELT CANDLE ORNAMENT

You will need: $4^1/_2$" x 12" rectangle of red felt; pinking shears; tracing paper; scraps of yellow, red, and green felt; $^1/_4$"w double-fold black bias tape; 1" dia. wooden button; brown felt-tip pen; 3"w wooden star cutout; $^3/_8$" dia. red button; spring-type clothespin; and a hot glue gun and glue sticks.

1. Trim one short edge of red felt rectangle with pinking shears. Beginning at short unpinked edge, roll rectangle to form candle; glue to secure.

2. Trace large flame, small flame, and holly leaf patterns (pg. 180) onto tracing paper. Use patterns to cut one large flame from yellow felt and one small flame from red felt. Center red flame at bottom of yellow flame; glue in place. Use pattern to cut two holly leaves from green felt.

3. Cut one 6" and two 3" lengths of bias tape. Glue 6" length along edge of yellow flame. Glue one 3" length to each leaf.

4. Glue wooden button to center front of candle over pinked edge.

5. Glue bottom of flame to center top of candle.

6. Use pen to draw dots along edges of wooden star. Glue candle to center of star.

7. Arrange leaves at base of candle; glue in place. Glue red button to point of one leaf.

8. Glue clothespin to bottom of wooden star.

Dressed for holiday fun, our gingerbread girl is a fresh and folksy way to put a homespun touch on the tree, a present, or an evergreen garland. Made by lightly stuffing two layers of craft paper, this little miss sports a fused-fabric dress and a curly wire hanger decorated with buttons and bows.

GINGERBREAD GIRL ORNAMENT
You will need: tracing paper, two 5¹/₂" x 8" rectangles of brown craft paper, paper-backed fusible web, scraps of assorted fabrics, black pen, red colored pencil, polyester fiberfill, three assorted buttons, 16" length of floral wire, and craft glue.

1. Trace outline only of gingerbread girl pattern (pg. 184) onto tracing paper; cut out. Use pattern to cut two shapes from paper rectangles.

2. Referring to *Fusing Basics* (pg. 187), use body, dress, collar, button, foot, tree, tree trunk, and cuff patterns (pg. 184) to make appliqués from assorted fabrics. Arrange appliqués on one paper shape; fuse in place.

3. Use pen to draw face, cheeks, and leg line on gingerbread girl. Use red pencil to color cheeks.

4. Glue edges of paper shapes together, leaving opening for stuffing. Stuff ornament lightly with fiberfill; glue opening closed.

5. Thread buttons onto floral wire, loosely curling sections of wire between buttons by wrapping around pencil. Insert ends of wire through shoulders of ornament and bend ends to secure.

6. Tear four ¹/₂" x 2" strips of fabric. Knot three lengths around wire. For hair bow, knot center of remaining fabric strip; glue in place.

IN ONLY 30 MINUTES!

*W*hat a wondrous delight! These fancy ornaments glitter and gleam with gold, red, and green jewels. And surprisingly enough, you can make one in just a half-hour! Pearled gold dimensional paint adds sparkle to our filigree designs, which are cut from clear plastic.

FILIGREE ORNAMENTS

For each ornament, you will need: clear shrink-art plastic; removable tape; assorted gold, red, and green acrylic jewels; tacky glue; pearlized gold dimensional paint; hole punch; and an 8" length of ¼"w gold ribbon.

1. Place plastic directly over desired ornament pattern (pg. 184 or 185); tape in place.

2. Referring to pattern for placement, glue jewels to plastic.

3. Apply paint onto plastic over lines of pattern and around jewels; allow to dry.

4. Cut out ornament along outer edge of design.

5. Punch a hole at top of ornament.

6. For hanger, thread ribbon through hole, matching ends; tie in a knot.

BUTTONED-UP PHOTO ORNAMENT

IN ONLY **3:1** MINUTES!

Showcase a precious portrait in this unique frame ornament embellished with an assortment of gold buttons. Foam core board wrapped in gold ribbon provides the base for this elegant project, and a darling picture gives it extra charm.

GOLD BUTTON FRAME ORNAMENT

You will need: drawing compass, 4" square of foam core board, craft knife, 1 yd. of $^{7}/_{8}$"w gold satin ribbon, 3" square of poster board, desired photo, assorted gold buttons, $^{3}/_{8}$ yd. of $1^{3}/_{8}$"w gold mesh ribbon, $^{1}/_{2}$ yd. of $^{1}/_{4}$"w gold mesh ribbon, and a hot glue gun and glue sticks.

1. For frame, use compass to draw a $3^{1}/_{4}$" dia. circle on foam core board. Draw a $1^{3}/_{4}$" circle in center of $3^{1}/_{4}$" circle. Use craft knife to cut out frame.

2. Wrap frame with gold satin ribbon to cover completely; glue ends in place.

3. Glue buttons to frame, overlapping to cover completely.

4. Draw a 3" dia. circle on poster board; cut out. Use poster board circle as a pattern to cut 3" circle from desired area of photo. Glue poster board circle to back of photo circle. Center photo on back of frame and glue in place.

5. Tie $1^{3}/_{8}$"w gold mesh ribbon into a bow; trim ends.

6. For hanger, fold $^{1}/_{4}$"w mesh ribbon in half. Tie a knot $1^{3}/_{4}$" from fold. Glue bow to knot. Glue streamers to back of frame ornament.

Heartwarming images of Kris Kringle, snipped from gift wrap, give our antique-look tree-trimmer a nostalgic look. Gold beads, ribbon, and a tassel add the final touches to the quick 14-minute project.

WOODEN SANTA BLOCK ORNAMENT

You will need: three 1½" square wooden blocks, Santa-pattern gift wrap, decoupage glue, craft knife, wood-tone spray, 12" length of ³⁄₈"w gold ribbon, gold spray paint, two 1" dia. wooden beads, gold tassel, and a hot glue gun and glue sticks.

1. Place blocks together end to end. Cut four different Santa figures from gift wrap. Use decoupage glue to glue one Santa to each side of blocks, overlapping at corners if necessary; allow glue to dry. To separate blocks, use craft knife to cut paper between blocks.

2. Lightly spray blocks with wood-tone spray; allow to dry.

3. Cut two 1" pieces of ribbon. Center and hot glue one end of one piece to top of center block and one end of remaining piece to bottom of center block. Glue remaining end of top strip to bottom of top block; glue remaining end of bottom strip to top of bottom block.

4. Spray paint beads gold; allow to dry.

5. Cut a 2" strip of ribbon. Thread tassel loop through one bead; thread ribbon through loop of tassel. Glue ends of ribbon to bottom of bottom block.

6. Cut two 8" lengths of ribbon; fold one length in half. Glue ends to top of top block. Thread bead onto folded ribbon; tie a knot in ribbon at top of bead.

7. Tie remaining 8" length of ribbon into a bow; glue to top of ornament near hanger.

SOFT-TOUCH SNOWMAN

IN ONLY
15
MINUTES!

Even before the first flurries fall, you can have fun building a jaunty snowman ornament. A white terry washcloth wrapped around a foam ball creates the look of snow. Felt features and a toy top hat give this fellow his jolly personality.

TERRY SNOWMAN

You will need: 3" dia. foam ball, white terry washcloth, rubber band, tracing paper, scraps of orange and black felt, $1/8$"w red satin ribbon for hanger and bow, small top hat to fit foam ball, $1/4$"w red grosgrain ribbon for hatband, three small artificial holly berries, and a hot glue gun and glue sticks.

1. For head, center foam ball on washcloth. Wrap washcloth tightly around ball and secure with rubber band. Cut off excess washcloth.

2. Trace nose pattern (pg. 184) onto tracing paper; cut one shape from orange felt. Roll nose into a cone shape and glue to secure.

3. Cut eight small pieces of black felt for eyes and mouth. Glue nose, mouth pieces, and eyes to head.

4. For hanger, cut a 9" length of satin ribbon; glue ends to top of hat, forming a loop. Tie a 6" length of satin ribbon into a small bow; glue over ends of hanger.

5. Glue hatband and holly berries to hat. Glue hat to snowman head, covering rubber band and raw edges of washcloth.

It's Christmas!
time to trim the tree,
wrap the gifts,
Bake the cookies
And Spend time
with Friends

Gifts FOR ALL

The weather outside is frightful but the pics inside are delightful!!

Pics of me trimming the tree

Tired of giving the same old stodgy neckties and fuzzy slippers? This year, you can create gifts that will get "two thumbs up" from everyone on your list. Your favorite shutterbugs will love stashing seasonal photos in a holiday memory album or kid-friendly picture book. A friendship sampler is a sentimental treasure. And who could resist a mistletoe hat that says "Kiss Me!!"? Grab your glue gun and get started early; you'll want to make these great gifts for everyone you know!

FIRESIDE WRAP

Who doesn't enjoy curling up by the fire on a cold winter night! This handsome blanket is perfect for snuggling, and it's super simple to make with no machine sewing.

WHAT TO BUY

1$\frac{1}{2}$ yds. of 54"w wool plaid fabric, ecru and red felt pieces, and red embroidery floss

THINGS YOU HAVE AT HOME

Thread, tracing paper, and an embroidery needle

FESTIVE WOOL BLANKET

Refer to Embroidery Stitches, page 189, before beginning project. Use four strands of floss for all stitching.

1. Cut selvages from fabric. Sew 1$\frac{1}{2}$" from edges of fabric. Pull threads to fringe all edges of fabric to stitching line.

2. Trace patterns, page 153, onto tracing paper. Using patterns, cut two mittens and two flower centers from ecru felt and two cuffs and two flowers from red felt. Arrange shapes on one corner of blanket; pin in place.

3. Work Blanket Stitch around edges of cuffs, mittens, and flowers. Work Straight Stitch and Cross Stitch in flower centers.

ELEGANT WELCOME

Surprise a friend with this fragrant wreath to greet the season. Our economical project combines the elegant look of shimmering gold ribbon with the delicate scent of potpourri for a unique Yuletide accent.

WHAT TO BUY

$3/4$" x $8^7/8$" dia. foam wreath, $1/4$ yd. of fabric, potpourri, $5/8$ yd. of $1^1/2$"w gold ribbon, and 3 yds. of $1/4$"w gold trim

THINGS YOU HAVE AT HOME

6" length of floral wire and a hot glue gun

POTPOURRI WREATH

1. Tear fabric into seven $1^1/4$" x 44" strips. Wrap strips around wreath, gluing ends to secure.

2. Glue potpourri onto wreath, covering front and sides.

3. Tie gold ribbon into a bow. Cut a 27" length of trim; tie into a bow. Glue trim bow to knot of ribbon bow.

4. Wrap remaining trim around wreath; glue in place. Glue bows to top of wreath.

5. For hanger, bend floral wire in half; glue ends to top back of wreath.

TWO THUMBS UP

*Y*ou'll get "two thumbs up" when you give a pair of these warm-and-snuggly fleece mittens adorned with felt appliqués and buttons. Choose bright colors to reflect the fun of the season!

WHAT TO BUY
Green Mittens:
Green fleece mittens; white felt piece; white, orange, green, and black embroidery floss; and twelve ³/₈" dia. white buttons

Red Mittens:
Red fleece mittens, green and black felt pieces, ecru and green embroidery floss, and a package of assorted craft buttons

THINGS YOU HAVE AT HOME
Cardboard, tracing paper, and an embroidery needle

FESTIVE HOLIDAY MITTENS
Refer to Embroidery Stitches, page 189, before beginning project. Use three strands of floss for all stitching. To prevent catching back of mitten while stitching, place a piece of cardboard inside mitten.

(Continued on page 147)

HERE COMES SANTA CLAUS!

There'll be no doubt Santa's on his way when folks see baby in this adorable holiday romper! Using only a few paints, it's simple to embellish a store-bought outfit for a little one.

WHAT TO BUY
infant-size red romper and flesh and green acrylic paint

THINGS YOU HAVE AT HOME
Waxed paper, tracing paper, transfer paper, paintbrushes, white and black acrylic paint, and a black permanent fabric marker

SANTA ROMPER
1. Place a sheet of waxed paper inside romper.

2. Referring to making patterns, page 187, trace pattern, page 154, onto tracing paper. Transfer pattern to front of romper.

3. Paint Santa design. Use marker to outline painted design and hat. Use white paint to create swirls for beard, paint dots on hat, and highlight eyes.

"STAMP" OF APPROVAL

*T*his holiday frame is sure to receive a "stamp" of approval! Use sandpaper to give a timeworn look to a wooden frame, then glue postage stamps and card stock strips to the borders. Special tidings written with a gold paint pen finish the project.

WHAT TO BUY
Wooden frame, gold and brown acrylic paint, and four Christmas stamps

THINGS YOU HAVE AT HOME
Paintbrush, sandpaper, card stock to match stamps, decorative-edge craft scissors, craft glue, gold paint pen, and acrylic spray sealer

POSTAGE STAMP FRAME
1. Referring to *Painting Basics*, page 188, paint frame brown; allow to dry. Lightly sand with sandpaper. Dry-brush frame with gold paint.

2. Adhere stamps to card stock and use craft scissors to cut out 1/4" outside edges of stamp.

3. Cut one strip of card stock slightly shorter and narrower than each side of frame. Glue strips and stamps to frame.

4. Write desired message with pen. Spray frame with sealer.

YULETIDE MEMORIES

*G*ive a friend's Yuletide photos the attention they deserve on these festive memory pages! They're perfect backdrops for unforgettable moments.

WHAT TO BUY
Three sheets of acid-free decorative paper and three sheets of white, red, or green card stock

THINGS YOU HAVE AT HOME
Scissors, decorative-edge craft scissors, scrapbook album pages, glue stick, photographs, items to decorate pages (we used Christmas card cutouts and motifs, stickers, and scraps of paper), and a black permanent fine-point marker

MEMORY PAGES
When the archival quality of greeting cards or other materials is unknown, you may want to use a deacidifcation spray or other preservation safeguards.

1. For each page, use decorative-edge craft scissors to trim acid-free paper to fit album page. Glue paper to page.

2. Select desired photographs for each page. Use scissors or craft scissors to cut desired images from photographs.

3. Mat images by gluing to card stock and trimming $1/8$" to $1/2$" outside edge of images or by "framing" with cutouts from Christmas cards.

4. Arrange and glue matted photographs to pages. Add desired decorations to pages.

5. Use marker to write desired captions on each page.

SNOW FRIENDS

Hugged by a friendly snow couple, this basket will hold candy, Christmas cards, or odds and ends in wintertime style! The pleasant pals are made from socks and "dressed" in scraps of fabric.

WHAT TO BUY

One pair each of women's white and red socks with ribbing, 5mm black flat-back beads, $1/8$" dia. red pom-poms, and an oval basket (we used a 7" x $10^1/_4$" basket)

THINGS YOU HAVE AT HOME

Polyester fiberfill; thread; red and black embroidery floss; embroidery needle; tracing paper; jute twine; drawing compass; scraps of lace trim, black felt, and fabric; and a hot glue gun

SNOW FRIENDS BASKET

Refer to Embroidery Stitches, page 189, before beginning project.

1. For each head, cut 3" from toe end of one white sock; set aside remainder. Stuff sock toe pieces with fiberfill. Hand sew openings closed.

2. For each face, glue two beads to head for eyes. Glue a pom-pom to each face for nose. Use three strands of black floss to work Stem Stitch for mouths.

3. For arms, cut ribbing from remainder of each sock; cut ribbing in half lengthwise. Matching right sides and long edges, sew $1/8$" from long edge and along one end of each arm, forming a tube; turn right side out. Stuff each arm with fiberfill. Hand sew opening closed.

4. Trace pattern, page 159, onto tracing paper. Using pattern, cut eight mittens from felt. Leaving straight edge open, use one strand of red floss and work Blanket Stitch to sew each pair of mitten shapes together. Lightly stuff each mitten with fiberfill. Glue one mitten over hand-sewn end of each arm.

(Continued on page 149)

REINDEER TREATS

Santa's favorite reindeer can't wait to deliver sweet treats to your friends! You'll want to make a whole herd of whimsical reindeer!

WHAT TO BUY
4" dia. glass ivy bowl, brown chenille stems, ²/₃ yd. of ¹/₄"w red ribbon, 15mm wiggle eyes, red craft foam, and two 5.5-oz. bags of candy

THINGS YOU HAVE AT HOME
Scraps of natural raffia, black permanent felt-tip marker, and a hot glue gun

REINDEER CANDY BOWL
1. Cut two 8" and two 5" lengths of chenille stems. Twist one 5" length around each 8" length. Bend stems to make antlers. Glue one antler to each side of bowl.

2. Cut several 1¹/₄" lengths of raffia; center between antlers and glue just below rim of bowl.

3. Tie ribbon into a bow around rim of bowl, covering top ends of raffia.

4. For nose, cut a 1" dia. circle from craft foam. Glue nose and eyes to front of bowl, just below raffia.

5. Use marker to draw eyebrows and mouth on bowl.

6. Place candy in bowl.

FUNNY-FACE SNOWMAN

Looking for a an original (but economical) way to package your home-baked goodies? Then you'll love our funny-face snowman gift bags! For next to nothing, you can transform lunch sacks into creative characters.

WHAT TO BUY
White paper lunch bags (package of 50), white and black craft foam sheets, white paper doilies (package of 20), and two yds. of 1½"w wired ribbon

THINGS YOU HAVE AT HOME
Drawing compass, ¼" dia. hole punch, scrap of pink construction paper, black felt-tip pen, jumbo craft stick, assorted small black buttons, and a hot glue gun

SNOWMAN GIFT BAGS

1. For each snowman head, use compass to draw a 2¼" dia. circle on white craft foam; cut out. Punch two holes from pink paper for cheeks; glue in place on face. Use pen to draw eyes and mouth.

2. For hat, cut a ½" x 2½" rectangle and a 1½" square from black craft foam. Arrange hat pieces on snowman head; glue in place.

3. For arms, draw around craft stick on white craft foam; cut out.

4. For snowflakes, cut small shapes from doilies. Glue snowflakes to bag and hat. Glue buttons to bag.

5. Place gift in bag.

6. Fold each side of bag top toward center to form a point. Position arms at point and roll top of bag and arms down twice; glue in place. Glue head and hat to center top of bag.

7. For scarf, tie ribbon around snowman neck.

FUN ON THE GO

These festive characters are ready for fun on the go! Our felt Santas and gingerbread boy are simply fused to a plain canvas tote and edged with quaint blanket stitching for a fast finish.

WHAT TO BUY

13" x 17" white canvas tote bag; one white, one flesh, one tan, and two red felt pieces; red and black embroidery floss; four black beads; white baby rickrack; $\frac{1}{2}$"w green satin ribbon (10-yd. spool); and $\frac{1}{8}$"w green satin ribbon (10-yd. spool)

THINGS YOU HAVE AT HOME

Tracing paper, paper-backed fusible web, scrap of black felt, pinking shears, embroidery needle, thread, scrap of red ribbon, assorted white buttons, 1"w paper-backed fusible web tape, scrap of Christmas print fabric, and a hot glue gun

FUN FELT CANVAS TOTE BAG

Before beginning project, refer to Embroidery Stitches, page 189. Use six strands of floss for all stitching.

1. Matching short edges, fold tan felt piece in half; cut along fold. Fuse tan felt pieces together; fuse red felt pieces together.

2. Trace Santa, boots, and gingerbread boy patterns, page 158, onto tracing paper; cut out. Draw around gingerbread boy pattern on tan felt; draw around Santa pattern two times on red felt. Using

boots pattern, cut two shapes from black felt. Cut out Santas. Use pinking shears to cut out gingerbread boy.

3. Carefully separate layers of felt at bottom of each Santa body. Position boots between layers; pin in place.

4. Use black floss to work Blanket Stitch around edges of Santas, French Knots for eyes, and Straight Stitch for noses. Use red floss to work Backstitch for

gingerbread boy mouth. Sew beads to gingerbread boy for eyes.

5. Follow *Fusing Basics*, page 187, and use patterns, page 158, to make two each of beard, mustache, and pom-pom appliqués, and four cuff appliqués, using pinking shears to cut out cuffs and pom-poms. Arrange appliqués on each Santa; fuse into place.

(Continued on page 148)

ARTFUL ALBUM

An ordinary greeting card provides the centerpiece for this artful photo album. Festive print fabric is used to cover the padded frame and make the easy-to-fuse appliqués. Even better, this gift is a real pocketbook pleaser!

WHAT TO BUY

$10^1/4$" x $11^1/2$" photo album, $1/3$ yd. of green fabric, and a red felt piece

THINGS YOU HAVE AT HOME

Tracing paper, corrugated cardboard, scraps of red and green fabrics and batting, pinking shears, paper-backed fusible web, spray adhesive, 4" x 6" or larger greeting card, and a hot glue gun

HOLIDAY PHOTO ALBUM

1. Referring to *Making Patterns,* page 187, trace frame pattern, page 162, onto tracing paper; cut out. Draw around pattern on cardboard, batting, felt, and wrong side of purchased green fabric. Cut out cardboard and batting shapes along drawn lines. Use spray adhesive to attach batting to cardboard. Cut out fabric frame 1" outside drawn lines. Use pinking shears to cut out felt frame $1/4$" outside drawn lines.

2. Follow *Fusing Basics,* page 187, and use patterns, page 162, to make eight (four in reverse) leaf and seventeen berry appliqués from fabric scraps. Arrange appliqués at least $1^1/4$" from edges of green fabric frame; fuse in place.

3. Clip inner and outer corners of appliquéd fabric to within $1/4$" of drawn lines (Fig. 1).

Fig. 1

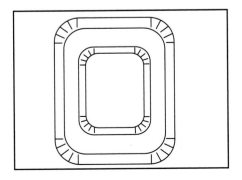

4. Apply spray adhesive to wrong side of appliquéd fabric. Center batting side of cardboard frame on wrong side of fabric. Smooth edges of fabric to back of cardboard frame; glue in place.

5. Center card in opening of felt frame; hot glue edges in place. Center felt frame with photo on album front; hot glue in place. Repeat to glue appliquéd frame over felt frame.

6. Fuse two $1^1/2$" x $16^1/2$" scraps of red fabric together. Use pinking shears to cut a 1" x 16" strip from fused fabric. Tie strip into a bow; glue to album.

CREATIVE THANK-YOU'S

*E*xpress your "thanks" and recycle favorite Christmas cards at the same time! Patterned tissue paper provides a backdrop for the festive motifs, which are glued to inexpensive note cards. Scraps of ribbon and greenery add the finishing touches.

WHAT TO BUY
4" x 5" note cards with envelopes

THINGS YOU HAVE AT HOME
Assorted tissue paper, craft glue, glue stick, Christmas cards, red and black permanent fine-point markers, and scraps of ribbon, and artificial greenery

THANK-YOU CARDS

Use glue stick for all gluing unless otherwise indicated.

1. For each card, tear a piece of tissue paper large enough to cover desired area on front of card. Glue tissue paper to card. If desired, glue a second piece of torn tissue paper or torn tissue paper strips to front or inside of card.

2. Cut desired motifs from Christmas cards. Glue motifs over tissue paper on front of card.

3. Use markers to write message on front or inside of card.

4. Tie a length of ribbon into a bow. Use craft glue to attach bow and greenery to card.

FUN PHOTO KEEPERS

Youngsters will have a ball decorating these photo books to give to their friends! Grown-ups can help cover plain albums with scraps cut from paper grocery bags, then let the kids add handwritten messages and trims cut from scrapbook paper. What fun (and inexpensive) gifts!

WHAT TO BUY
Two 5" x 7" photo books and seven assorted sheets of scrapbook paper

THINGS YOU HAVE AT HOME
Brown paper grocery bags, spray adhesive, tracing paper, 1/4" dia. hole punch, black felt-tip pen, and craft glue

KIDS' PHOTO BOOKS
1. For photo book cover, draw around open book on grocery bag; cut 1/2" outside drawn line.

2. Clipping corners and folding edges to inside of photo book, use spray adhesive to glue cover in place. Cut two 5" x 6" pieces from paper bag; glue to inside front and back covers of photo book.

3. Piecing as necessary, cut 3/8"w strips of decorative scrapbook paper; glue in place along borders of photo book.

4. Trace patterns, page 168, onto tracing paper. Using patterns, cut tree and snowman from scrapbook paper. For tree "ornaments," punch holes from desired colors of paper. Glue shapes onto front of book.

5. Use pen to write desired message and draw details.

HANDMADE GREETINGS

*S*end your Yuletide wishes on special greeting cards you make yourself. Blank note cards and envelopes are transformed into gift-shop-quality stationery using holiday stickers along with materials you probably already have at home, such as fabric scraps, buttons, and raffia.

WHAT TO BUY
4" x 5" note cards with envelopes, package of assorted holiday stickers, and a sheet of colored card stock

THINGS YOU HAVE AT HOME
Scraps of fabric, white and decorative paper, corrugated cardboard, paper-backed fusible web, and raffia; decorative-edge craft scissors; tracing paper; assorted buttons; black permanent fine-point pen; drawing compass; and a hot glue gun

HANDMADE CHRISTMAS CARDS
Refer to photo and use the following suggestions to decorate cards.

1. Use craft scissors to cut borders or frames from card stock.

2. Refer to *Fusing Basics*, page 187, and use fabric and patterns, page 161, to make appliqués. Fuse in place on cards.

3. Use raffia bows, stickers, and written messages to decorate cards as desired.

GREAT GIFT BAGS

For a truly festive presentation, pack your gifts in these economical bags embellished with plastic canvas needlework. Whether you choose the Santa, snowman, or tree — or all three — these whimsical totes will make your gifts doubly delightful!

WHAT TO BUY

White, flesh, pink, red, blue, light green, green, and grey 3-ply sport-weight yarn; three 10" x 13" sheets of 10 mesh plastic canvas; red and green embroidery floss; red and green curling ribbon; and tissue paper

THINGS YOU HAVE AT HOME

#16 tapestry needle, black yarn, and a hot glue gun

PLASTIC CANVAS GIFT BAGS

Refer to Plastic Canvas, page 190, before beginning project.

1. For Santa ornament, cut a piece of plastic canvas measuring 28 x 31 threads. To stitch design, refer to chart and color key, page 157.

2. For Christmas tree ornament, cut a piece of plastic canvas measuring 28 x 32 threads. To stitch design, refer to chart and color key, page 157.

3. For snowman ornament, cut a piece of plastic canvas measuring 28 x 31 threads. To stitch design, refer to chart and color key, page 157.

4. For front and back of each gift bag, cut two pieces of plastic canvas measuring 44 x 48 threads. For sides, cut two pieces of plastic canvas measuring 22 x 48 threads. For handle, cut a piece of plastic canvas measuring 8 x 107 threads. For bottom, cut one piece of plastic canvas measuring 22 x 44 threads. Use white yarn for all joining.

5. Center one ornament on front of bag and glue in place.

6. Place tissue in bag. Cut 30" lengths of red and green curling ribbon; place together and tie into a bow around handle.

MERRY BABY BIBS

Keep baby's dinnertime finery looking its best with our merry bibs. They're easy to make from purchased appliquéd guest towels, and at just a few dollars each, the price is right!

WHAT TO BUY
Two 11" x 17" appliquéd Christmas guest towels, double fold bias tape, and $1/2$" dia. hook and loop fasteners (package of six)

THINGS YOU HAVE AT HOME
Tracing paper, fabric marker, and thread

CHRISTMAS BABY BIBS

1. Trace neck opening pattern, page 165, onto tracing paper; cut out. Use fabric marker to draw around pattern on ends of towels opposite design; cut out.

2. Follow manufacturer's instructions to bind neck openings with bias tape.

3. Sew hook and loop fasteners on bibs.

CHRISTMAS IS COOL!

All in a row, friendly snowman faces trim this spirited sweatshirt that's just right for kids. Plaid fabric around the edge of the shirt creates "scarves" for the chilly guys, and a festive message wishes a "cool" Yule!

WHAT TO BUY
Blue sweatshirt (we used a child's size large), ¼ yd. of plaid fabric, white and orange felt pieces, white and black embroidery floss, and ³/₄" dia. white pom-poms

THINGS YOU HAVE AT HOME
Clear nylon thread, drawing compass, tracing paper, transfer paper, and assorted black buttons

SNOWMAN SWEATSHIRT
Refer to Embroidery Stitches, page 189, before beginning project. Use three strands of floss for all stitching.

1. Cut ribbing from bottom of sweatshirt. Measure around bottom of shirt; add 1½". Cut a strip of fabric 2¼" by the determined measurement.

2. Press short edges and one long edge of strip ½" to wrong side. Aligning raw edges, place right side of fabric strip on wrong side of shirt. Overlapping ends as necessary; pin in place. Use a ¼"w seam allowance to sew strip to shirt. Turn strip to right side of shirt; press. Topstitch long folded edge of strip to shirt.

3. For snowman head pattern, use compass to draw a 4" dia. circle on tracing paper. Using pattern, cut four heads from white felt; baste in place on shirt front. Follow *Stitching Appliqués,* page 187, to stitch heads in place.

4. Referring to *Making Patterns,* page 187, trace patterns, page 150, onto tracing paper. Transfer words onto shirt and smile to each snowman head.

5. Using white floss, work Running Stitch and French Knots for words and snowflakes. Sew pom-poms to shirt.

6. Use pattern to cut four noses from orange felt. Sew one nose to each snowman head. Sew buttons to heads for eyes. Use black floss to work smiles using Running Stitch and Cross Stitch.

7. For scarves, cut four 1¼" x 9" strips of fabric. Tie a knot in the center of each strip. Sew knot of one scarf beside each snowman.

DIMENSIONAL PORTRAIT

You won't believe how easy (and inexpensive) it is to create a gift-shop-quality accent like this one by simply layering Christmas card cutouts! The result is a unique 3-D portrait that comes to life before your eyes.

WHAT TO BUY
Box of Christmas cards with three alike, 4" x 5" piece of foam core board, poster board, 8" x 10" mat with precut opening to accommodate card, and an 8" x 10" frame with glass

THINGS YOU HAVE AT HOME
Craft glue

3-D CHRISTMAS PICTURE
1. For layers, cut desired shapes from two cards.

2. Cut small pieces from foam core board. Glue pieces onto back of each shape; glue shapes in layers onto remaining whole card.

3. Draw around outside of frame on poster board. Cut out 1/8" inside drawn line.

4. Center 3-D card on poster board piece; glue in place.

5. Insert mat behind glass; secure by bending frame staples over mat. Glue poster board with card to back of frame.

FRIENDSHIP SAMPLER

*T*his handmade sampler reminds us all of the special times that accompany the Christmas season. Bordered with a patchwork of fabric scraps and merry cutouts, the embroidered message is sure to delight a dear friend.

WHAT TO BUY
¹/₂ yd. of muslin; red, green, and brown embroidery floss; and an 11" x 14" frame

THINGS YOU HAVE AT HOME
Fabric marking pencil, paper-backed fusible web, scraps of assorted fabrics, tracing paper, craft knife, heavyweight cardboard, and a hot glue gun

CHRISTMAS SAMPLER
Refer to Embroidery Stitches, page 189, before beginning project. Use two strands of floss for all stitching.

1. For sampler background, cut two 13" x 16" pieces from muslin. Use marking pencil to draw a 9" x 11" rectangle in center of one background piece. Place background pieces together; pin in place.

2. For patchwork border, follow *Fusing Basics*, page 187, and make various lengths of 1"w rectangle appliqués from fabric scraps. Align appliqués outside drawn lines of rectangle on background piece; fuse in place.

3. Trace pattern for sampler, page 167, onto tracing paper. Center pattern inside fused border; pin in place. Stitching through pattern, use Backstitch, French

Knots, Stem Stitch, and Running Stitch to embroider design on sampler. Carefully tear away pattern.

4. Use patterns, page 167, and remaining fabric scraps to make tree, star, heart, gingerbread man, circle, and present appliqués. Arrange appliqués around saying; fuse in place.

5. Use craft knife to cut an 11" x 14" piece of cardboard. Center sampler on cardboard, wrapping edges to back; glue in place. Glue sampler to back of frame.

MEMORIES TO TREASURE

*T*his clever keeper offers a friend an elegant place to tuck away holiday memories. Our handsome memory box features a padded lid accented with a lattice of golden cord. The roomy box can hold snapshots, mementos, and more!

WHAT TO BUY
$7^1/_2$" x 11" red craft storage box, gold acrylic paint, $^1/_2$ yd. of Christmas print fabric, and gold cord (9-ft spool)

THINGS YOU HAVE AT HOME
Natural sponge, batting, four buttons, pushpin, clear nylon thread, and a hot glue gun

MEMORY BOX
1. Referring to *Painting Basics*, page 188, use gold paint to sponge paint box bottom; allow to dry.

2. Cut an $11^1/_2$" x 15" rectangle from batting. Cut a $1^1/_2$" square from each corner. Glue batting to top and sides of box lid.

(Continued on page 147)

"SPEC-TACULAR" GIFT

Imagine the delight in someone's eyes when you deliver this sweet surprise — Mrs. Claus all decked out in wire spectacles and a nightcap made from a doily. Fill her with treats for a "spec-tacular" gift!

WHAT TO BUY
4" dia. glass ivy bowl, two 5.5-oz. bags of candy, 9$\frac{1}{2}$" dia. doily, $\frac{2}{3}$ yd. of $\frac{1}{4}$"w red ribbon, 15mm wiggle eyes, red craft foam, white curly craft hair, and one pair of 3$\frac{1}{2}$"w doll glasses

THINGS YOU HAVE AT HOME
Poster board, polyester fiberfill, rubber band, tracing paper, and craft glue

MRS. SANTA CANDY DISH
1. Draw around rim of bowl on poster board; cut out.

2. Place candy in bowl. Glue a ball of fiberfill to poster board circle. Place circle fiberfill side up on bowl.

3. For hat, center doily over fiberfill; secure around rim of bowl with rubber band. Tie ribbon into a bow around rim, covering rubber band.

4. Trace pattern, page 156, onto tracing paper; cut out. Using pattern, cut one mouth from craft foam. Glue eyes and mouth to bowl; glue hair to bowl under rim of hat.

5. Hook temples of glasses into lace of doily to hold in place over eyes.

WANTED: ONE JOLLY ELF!

*T*his jolly little elf is "slated" for stardom! Using craft foam and paints, you can transform an inexpensive chalkboard into a cherished holiday gift for a youngster.

WHAT TO BUY

5⅝" x 7⅝" chalkboard with wooden frame; white, red, and green acrylic paint; peach, red, and green craft foam; ½" dia. jingle bell; and a roll of ½"w self-adhesive magnetic strip

THINGS YOU HAVE AT HOME

Paintbrushes, tracing paper, transfer paper, black felt-tip pen, blush for cheeks, jute twine, and a hot glue gun

ELF CHALKBOARD

Allow paint to dry after each color application.

1. Paint red and green rectangles along frame of chalkboard.

2. Trace patterns, page 150, onto tracing paper. Follow *Making Patterns*, page 187, to transfer message onto frame of chalkboard; paint words white. Paint white dots on frame. Use pen to draw around letters, draw designs on circles, and draw lines between rectangles.

(Continued on page 147)

CUSTOM GIFT BASKETS

*I*nstead of delivering your Christmas goodies in plain paper bags, transform ordinary baskets into custom carriers for your treats! Simply wrap a basket in homespun fabric, add a little padding, and tie off with jute. Holly leaves and berries cut from felt add the finishing touches.

WHAT TO BUY
5" dia. basket, ¹/₂ yd. of fabric, and red green felt pieces

THINGS YOU HAVE AT HOME
¹/₂"w paper-backed fusible web tape, rubber band, polyester fiberfill, jute rope, tracing paper, wire cutters, floral wire, thread, and a hot glue gun

FABRIC-COVERED BASKET
1. Measure basket from one side of rim to opposite side of rim (Fig. 1); multiply by 1¹/₂ and add ¹/₂" (this will be diameter of fabric circle). Cut a square of fabric 2" larger than the determined diameter.

Fig. 1

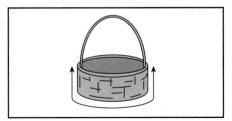

2. Follow *Cutting a Fabric Circle*, page 191, to cut a circle the determined diameter. Fuse web tape to wrong side of fabric around edge of circle. Turn edge ¹/₂" to wrong side; fuse in place.

3. Center basket on wrong side of fabric circle. Bring edges of fabric up and secure around rim of basket with rubber band; adjust gathers evenly.

4. Tuck fiberfill between fabric and sides of basket for desired fullness.

5. Tie a 25" length of jute into a knot around basket, covering rubber band. Knot ends of jute.

6. Trace patterns, page 158, onto tracing paper. Using patterns, cut four holly leaves from green felt and three berries from red felt.

7. Cut two 2¹/₂" lengths of floral wire. Glue wires along center of two leaves. Glue remaining two leaves over wired leaves. Arrange leaves as desired.

8. Hand baste along edge of each berry; pull thread to gather slightly. Insert a small amount of fiberfill inside berry; pull thread tightly to gather around fiberfill. Knot and trim thread ends.

9. Glue leaves and berries over jute knot.

REINDEER DREAM TEAM

Even Santa couldn't beat these whimsical gift sacks! They're just the thing for bagging up small gifts for neighbors or co-workers. You can craft a whole team of reindeer.

WHAT TO BUY
Brown paper lunch bags (package of 50), three packages of 15mm oval wiggle eyes (three pair per package), three packages of $1^1/_2$" dia. pom-poms (three per package), and brown chenille stems

THINGS YOU HAVE AT HOME
Drawing compass, jute twine, scraps of fabric, and a hot glue gun

REINDEER GIFT BAGS
1. For each bag, fold top $3^1/_2$" of bag to front. Use compass to draw a 6" dia. half-circle on folded end of bag; cut along drawn line.

2. Cut a $4^1/_4$" length of jute; unravel slightly. Glue jute to fold of bag.

3. Cut a $^1/_2$" x 5" strip of fabric; tie into a bow. Glue bow to center of jute.

4. For face, glue eyes and pom-pom to bag.

5. Cut six 6" lengths of chenille stems. For each antler, twist two lengths around center of one length of chenille stem. Glue one end of each antler to inside top of bag.

CHRISTMAS KISSES

*T*he wearer of this merry cap will always be standing beneath the mistletoe at just the right moment! You can embellish a plain fleece hat with felt appliqués and simple stitches for practically nothing.

WHAT TO BUY
Fleece hat with folded brim, green felt piece, and white embroidery floss

THINGS YOU HAVE AT HOME
Tracing paper, embroidery needle, thread, and eight assorted white buttons

MISTLETOE HAT
Refer to Embroidery Stitches, page 189, before beginning project. Use six strands of floss for all stitching.

1. Trace patterns, page 151, onto tracing paper. Using patterns, cut three large leaves and four small leaves from felt.

2. Unfold brim of hat; turn hat wrong side out. With open end of hat at top, pin KISS ME!! pattern to brim of hat. Work Back Stitch and French Knots through pattern; carefully tear away pattern.

3. Turn hat right side out; refold brim. Sew mistletoe leaves and buttons to top and brim of hat.

ONE-HOUR GIFTS

Nothing compares to the pleasure of giving handmade gifts to special people. In this section, you'll find timesaving crafts for everyone on your list — and each project takes less than one hour! How about our dazzling decoupaged plates or a charming journal for a dear friend? Little girls will love our cute Christmas tree dress, and a beeswax candle will look great in anyone's window. Even though time is scarce during the holiday season, our quick collection makes it easy to create thoughtful tokens for your favorite folks.

IN ONLY
18
MINUTES!

*D*isplaying cherished photos *on bright memory album pages is a fun, creative way to remember those special holiday moments. Acid-free papers guarantee that precious snapshots will be protected from discoloring, and merry background papers add pizzazz.*

MEMORY ALBUM PAGES

You will need: tracing paper; transfer paper; stylus; yellow, parchment, and red acid-free paper; tree and star-shaped craft punches; hole punch; photos; acid-free Christmas papers; gold paint pen; acid-free album pages; colored pencils; pinking shears; black pen; and a glue stick.

1. Trace ornament A (pg. 183) and pull-toy horse (pg. 182) patterns onto tracing paper; cut out.

2. For ornament page, use pattern to cut one shape each from parchment and red paper.

3. Use punches to cut shapes from desired paper. Trim photo to fit center of ornament. Arrange cutouts and photo on Christmas paper; glue in place. Use gold paint pen to draw designs and ornament hanger on red ornament. Glue Christmas paper to album page.

4. For pull-toy horse page, use stylus to transfer pattern to parchment paper; cut out slightly outside drawn line. Use pencils to color design.

5. Use star punch to cut shapes from yellow paper.

6. For photo backgrounds, use pinking shears to cut red paper 3/8" larger all around than photos. Center photos on backgrounds and glue in place. Use pen to draw designs around borders.

7. Arrange photos, stars, and horse on Christmas paper and glue in place. Use black pen to draw pull string on horse. Glue Christmas paper to album page.

*E*lves aren't the only helpers Santa will have this Christmas! Dress up a youngster North-Pole style with a vibrant holiday smock. Easily fashioned by adding a felt collar and iron-on letters to a ready-made smock, this fun top will protect kids' clothes during the making and baking of the Yuletide season.

SANTA'S HELPER SMOCK

You will need: tracing paper, ¹/₃ yd. of green felt, child-size smock, red thread, red baby rickrack, ³/₄" red felt iron-on letters, red embroidery floss, and ¹/₂" dia. jingle bells.

1. Remove loop side of hook and loop fastener from smock; set aside.

2. Referring to *Making Patterns* (pg. 187), trace collar pattern (pg. 172) onto tracing paper. Use pattern to cut collar from felt. Sew collar to neckline of smock.

3. Cut a length of rickrack to fit around neckline. Sew rickrack in place over collar. Replace loop fastener over collar.

4. Cut an apostrophe shape from one spare letter. Arrange letters and apostrophe to spell SANTA'S HELPER on front of smock; follow manufacturer's instructions to fuse in place.

5. Use six strands of red embroidery floss to sew one jingle bell to each point of collar. Knot floss and trim ends, leaving ¹/₂" tails.

This whimsical snowman sweatshirt is a perfect warmer for chilly days — and it's oh-so-easy to make! Using clear nylon thread to stitch around the fused-on appliqués eliminates the need to change thread colors with each fabric. A pinned-on scarf gives a jaunty finish.

FROSTY SWEATSHIRT

You will need: paper-backed fusible web, scraps of white and black fabric and orange felt, sweatshirt, clear nylon thread, black embroidery floss, 1" dia. red button, two 3/4" dia. black buttons, white dimensional paint, 3" x 12" torn fabric strip for bow, and a safety pin.

1. Referring to *Fusing Basics* (pg. 187), use patterns (pg. 175) to make snowman head, nose, and hat appliqués. Arrange appliqués on sweatshirt front and fuse in place.

2. Use nylon thread and a narrow zigzag stitch to sew around edges of appliqués.

3. Referring to *Embroidery Stitches* (pg. 189), use black floss and work Straight Stitches for mouth on snowman. Sew red button on hat and black buttons on face for eyes.

4. Referring to *Painting Basics* (pg. 188), use dimensional paint to paint dots and snowflakes on sweatshirt front; allow to dry.

5. For scarf, tie knot at center of torn fabric strip. Use safety pin on wrong side of sweatshirt front to attach scarf.

CHRISTMAS CANDLE LIGHT

IN ONLY
15
MINUTES!

*F*olks on your gift list can add a touch of nostalgia to their homes with this charming beeswax candle lamp. Since the lamp is quick and easy to assemble (just 15 minutes for one lamp), plan on preparing a bunch for friends and relatives!

BEESWAX CANDLE LAMP

You will need: battery-powered candle lamp, honeycomb beeswax sheet, 24" length of 1³/₈"w ribbon, 2" length of floral wire, two 16" lengths of jute twine, and a small sprig of artificial greenery.

1. Measure height and circumference of candle; add 1" to circumference. Cut a piece of beeswax sheet the determined measurement. Wrap beeswax around candle, overlapping edges and pressing to seal.

2. Fold ribbon to form a double-loop bow; secure at center with wire. Trim ends of ribbon.

3. Using both lengths of jute twine, tie ribbon bow to base of candle; tie ends of jute into bow.

4. Insert end of greenery sprig into knot in jute.

Elegant yet easy to make, our festive wine glass provides a glamorous way to toast the holiday season! You can create this frosty effect in just 20 minutes — simply apply etching cream over star and dot stickers, then rinse! It's fun to fashion stemware for family members or create distinctive glassware for a favorite couple.

FINE WINE GLASS

You will need: a ¹/₈" hole punch, self-adhesive star stickers, wine glass, and etching cream.

1. Use hole punch to cut dots from self-adhesive sticker material between star stickers.

2. Apply star and dot stickers to glass.

3. Follow manufacturer's instructions to apply etching cream. Rinse glass; remove stickers.

WHITE CHRISTMAS GIFT BAG

*A*dd an air of enchantment to an extra-special present by tucking it in our elegant gift bag! Embellished with a lacy doily, gold berries, and charms, the outside of this lovely container will make friends and relatives eager to discover what's inside! It takes just over 20 minutes to turn a white gift bag into an eye-catching wrapper personalized with an embroidered monogram.

ELEGANT GIFT BAG

You will need: wrapping paper, white gift bag, gold paint pen, small crocheted or tatted doily, angel and heart-shaped charms, assorted buttons, assorted lace and braid trims, monogram letter, $1^1/2$ yds. of $1^1/2$"w white wired ribbon, gold berry sprigs, and a hot glue gun and glue sticks.

1. Cut a rectangle of wrapping paper $1/2$" smaller on all sides than front of gift bag. Center on front of bag; glue in place.

2. Use paint pen to draw a border $1/4$" outside edges of wrapping paper.

3. For flap, fold top 2" of bag to front.

4. Cut doily in half. Press $1/2$" of cut edge to wrong side of doily. Align folded edge of doily with folded edge at top of flap; glue doily in place.

5. Arrange trims, buttons, letter, and charms on front of gift bag; glue in place.

6. Referring to *Multi-Loop Bows* (pg. 191), tie ribbon into a multi-loop bow. Insert berries through knot in bow. Glue bow over doily near fold at top of flap.

7. Lift flap to place gift in bag.

JOLLY SNOWMEN GIFT BAGS

*B*undle your hard-to-wrap presents in our pretty yet practical gift carriers! It's amazingly easy to add jolly sponge-painted snowmen and perky grosgrain ribbon trim to sturdy brown shopping bags. In less than 30 minutes, your clever gift totes are ready to hold exciting surprises for special friends!

CHEERY GIFT BAGS

You will need: tracing paper; compressed craft sponge; white acrylic paint; paper plate; two 8" x 10" brown paper gift bags; white, red, orange, and brown dimensional paint; 16" length of red polka-dot grosgrain ribbon; and glue.

Note: Refer to *Painting Basics* (pg. 188) for all painting.

1. Trace large snowman pattern (pg. 174) onto tracing paper; cut out. Use pattern to cut shape from compressed sponge.

2. Use sponge and white acrylic paint to paint snowmen on bags; allow to dry.

3. Use dimensional paints to paint scarf, nose, buttons, face, and arms on each snowman. Use white dimensional paint to paint snow on bags.

4. Cut ribbon length in half; glue one half to top front edge of each bag.

*O*rdinary cork coasters become handy holiday helpers when they're decorated with holly motifs created with easy-to-use paint pens. They're inexpensive and super-quick to make, so you can craft sets for all your friends!

FESTIVE COASTERS
You will need: tracing paper; transfer paper; stylus; coasters with cork liners; white, red, and green paint pens; and clear acrylic spray sealer.

1. Trace holly with berries pattern (pg. 172) onto tracing paper. Use transfer paper and stylus to transfer design to each coaster.

2. Allowing to dry between coats, use paint pens to color designs.

3. Spray designs with one coat of sealer; allow to dry.

131

*H*ere's a nifty gift that's also a decorative place to stash things during the holidays. This papier-mâché box is a stellar hideaway for holiday snapshots, Christmas knickknacks, or candy. Fused-on fabric and basic painted designs make the project a snap to do.

STAR BOX

You will need: 12¹/₂"w star-shaped papier-mâché box, newspaper, red spray paint, 4"w wooden star, paintbrush, one 13" square each of paper-backed fusible web and Christmas print fabric, green acrylic paint, black medium-point marker, six ³/₄" dia. green buttons, and a hot glue gun and glue sticks.

1. Remove lid from box.

2. Place bottom of box upside down on newspaper. Use red spray paint to paint box bottom and wooden star; allow to dry.

3. Referring to *Fusing Basics* (pg. 187), fuse web to wrong side of fabric; do not remove paper backing. Place box lid on paper side of fused fabric; draw around lid. Cut out shape ¹/₄" inside drawn line. Center appliqué and fuse to box lid.

4. Use green paint to add stripes to sides of lid; allow to dry. Use marker to draw designs on sides of lid.

5. Center wooden star on lid; glue in place. Glue one button to each point of lid and one button to top of wooden star.

*M*ake any snack merrier by serving a warming beverage in one of these crafty cups. To quickly create the clever designs, use colored pencils to tint rubber-stamped images. Contrasting paper behind the punched stars or pinked edge provides a festive background.

FESTIVE MUGS

For each mug, you will need: rubber stamp; black ink pad; one piece of white cardstock and one piece of red or green cardstock, each measuring $3^1/_2$" x $10^1/_2$"; colored pencils; star punch or pinking shears; clear plastic coffee mug with insert; and a glue stick.

1. To make decorative mug liner, stamp white cardstock as desired; allow ink to dry. Use pencils to color designs.

2. Punch stars or use pinking shears to trim $^1/_2$" from bottom of white cardstock. Matching edges, glue decorated cardstock to red or green cardstock; allow to dry.

3. Remove insert from mug. Place liner inside mug and replace insert.

IN ONLY
45
MINUTES!

*S*noozing on our eye-catching pillowcases will inspire visions of light, lacy snowflakes dancing against the wintry sky. The dark green cases are edged with stenciled snowflakes and jumbo rickrack.

SNOWFLAKE PILLOWCASES

For each pillowcase, you will need: stencil plastic, craft knife, stencil brush, white fabric paint, dark green pillowcase, white jumbo rickrack, and white sewing thread.

1. Trace large and small snowflake patterns (pg. 172) onto stencil plastic. Use craft knife to cut out stencil segments along drawn lines.

2. Referring to *Painting Basics* (pg. 188), use stencil and fabric paint to paint snowflakes along hem of pillowcase; allow to dry.

3. Measure across end of pillowcase; add 1". Cut a length of rickrack the determined measurement. Turning ends of rickrack under $1/2$", sew rickrack to pillowcase along hem seam.

COZY SNOWMEN SWEATSHIRT

Sprinkle a festive frosting of holiday fun across the front of this dashing sweatshirt! To achieve the charming effect, sponge paint the snowmen, add accents using dimensional paints, and spatter paint the falling snow.

SNOWMEN SWEATSHIRT

You will need: tracing paper, compressed craft sponge, paper plate, white fabric paint, sweatshirt, toothbrush, paper towel, and assorted colors of dimensional paint.

Note: Refer to *Painting Basics* (pg. 188) for all painting.

1. Trace large snowman pattern (pg. 174) onto tracing paper; cut out. Use pattern to cut shape from sponge.

2. Use sponge shape to paint snowmen on front of sweatshirt; allow to dry.

3. Use dimensional paint to add faces, scarves, buttons, arms, and snow details to sweatshirt; allow to dry.

4. To spatter paint on sweatshirt, dip toothbrush bristles into fabric paint. Blot bristles on paper towel to remove excess paint. Holding toothbrush just above sweatshirt, pull thumb across bristles; allow paint to dry.

135

*S*anta's little helper will be as pretty as a Christmas tree when she wears this festive jumper! It's simple to "trim" a child's dress with rickrack "garland," fused-fabric ornaments, and perky plaid bows.

CHRISTMAS CUTIE'S DRESS

You will need: child's green fleece jumper, yellow baby rickrack, paper-backed fusible web, scraps of yellow and red fabrics, gold and red dimensional paint, 1⅓ yds. of 1½"w plaid ribbon, fabric glue, and three small safety pins.

1. Arrange rickrack on front of dress; glue in place.

2. Referring to *Fusing Basics* (pg. 187), use ball ornament and ornament top patterns (pg. 171) to make four appliqués each from red and yellow fabrics. Arrange appliqués on dress front and fuse in place.

3. Referring to *Painting Basics* (pg. 188), use gold dimensional paint to outline each ornament top and to draw hanger. Use red dimensional paint to outline each ornament.

4. Cut ribbon into three 15" lengths. Tie each length into a bow. Use safety pin on wrong side of dress to attach each bow to front of dress.

*O*ur versatile holiday basket has both decorative and practical appeal. Filled with pinecones, it's perfect as part of a Yuletide centerpiece. The fabric-wrapped basket can also be an extra-special holder for greeting cards or a charming way to deliver seasonal treats!

JINGLE BELL BASKET

You will need: woven basket, string, pencil, thumbtack, Christmas fabric, polyester fiberfill, large rubber band, pinking shears, $5/8$"w grosgrain ribbon, large jingle bell, and a hot glue gun and glue sticks.

1. Measure basket from rim to rim as shown in Fig. 1; multiply by $1^1/2$ to determine diameter of fabric circle. Cut a square of fabric 2" larger than the determined diameter.

Fig. 1

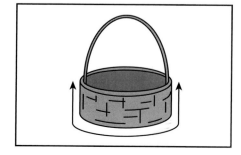

2. Use fabric square and follow *Cutting a Fabric Circle* (pg. 191) to cut a circle with the diameter determined in Step 1.

3. Center basket on wrong side of fabric circle. Bring edges of fabric up and secure around rim of basket with rubber band, adjusting gathers evenly. Tuck fiberfill into fabric around sides of basket for desired fullness.

4. Use pinking shears to trim fabric 1" above rim of basket.

5. Wrap ribbon around basket, covering rubber band; knot ribbon and trim ends.

6. Glue jingle bell to knot of ribbon.

*M*ake the season merrier for folks on your list by crafting colorful containers to hold tasty gifts. Holiday stickers and paint pens let you have a ball decorating these buckets in record time — just 10 minutes each — including the wired-ribbon bows on top!

TREAT BUCKETS

For each bucket, you will need:
Christmas stickers, plastic bucket with handle and lid, red and green paint pens, 1½ yds. of 1"w wired gingham ribbon, a hot glue gun and glue sticks, and desired treats.

1. Place stickers on bucket as desired. Use paint pens to add message, swirls, dots, and stars; allow to dry.

2. Cut a 20" length of ribbon; tie into a bow. Glue bow to handle; trim ends.

3. Fill bucket with treats.

*M*ini totes are terrific gifts for friends and neighbors — especially when they're filled with special treats! Using easy painting techniques and rickrack trim, you can decorate ready-made bags in no time.

GINGERBREAD MAN MINI TOTE

For each tote, you will need: green baby rickrack, green sewing thread, canvas mini tote bag, tracing paper, sharpened pencil with unused eraser, brown and red acrylic paint, paintbrushes, and white dimensional paint.

1. Cut two pieces of rickrack the same length as tote handle; sew one length along center of each handle.

2. Trace gingerbread man and heart patterns (pg. 173) onto tracing paper; cut out. Use pencil to draw around patterns on front of tote.

3. Paint gingerbread men brown and heart red. Use pencil eraser dipped in red paint to stamp dots on tote. Allow paint to dry.

4. Referring to *Painting Basics* (pg. 188), use dimensional paint to add details to gingerbread men; allow to dry.

With a multitude of uses, this charming gingerbread footstool is as handy as it is decorative! Simple painting techniques and fabric appliqués make this project a darling addition to any Yuletide home.

HOLIDAY FOOTSTOOL

You will need: fine grit sandpaper; tack cloth; unfinished wooden footstool; sponge paintbrush; white, green, and tan matte-finish paint; sponge piece; paper-backed fusible web; ¼ yd. of fabric with Christmas motifs; and acrylic spray sealer.

1. Use sandpaper to lightly sand surface of stool; use tack cloth to remove dust.

2. Applying two coats and allowing to dry between coats, paint top of stool tan. Paint base and legs of stool green.

3. Referring to *Painting Basics* (pg. 188), use a sponge piece to lightly stamp edge of stool top with green paint; allow to dry. Lightly stamp all edges of stool with white paint.

4. Refer to *Fusing Basics* (pg. 187) to make appliqués using Christmas motifs from fabric.

5. Arrange appliqués on top and legs of stool; fuse in place.

6. Spray stool with sealer.

This embellished box will keep goodies safe for Santa! The background fabric and cookie motifs are fused to the top of a papier-mâché box, and the "icing" details are added with dimensional paint. The jolly elf will find a sweet surprise when he peeks inside!

SANTA'S COOKIE BOX

You will need: 6" square papier-mâché box, paper-backed fusible web, scraps of assorted fabrics, parchment paper, hole punch, red embroidery floss, pinking shears, ³/₄"w fusible web tape, black felt-tip pen, white and brown dimensional paint, and glue.

1. Referring to *Fusing Basics* (pg. 187), use gingerbread man, tag, heart, and cookie patterns (pg. 173) to make appliqués from desired fabric scraps.

2. For paper tag, cut 3" x 4" pieces of parchment paper and fusible web. Fuse web to wrong side of paper; do not remove paper backing. Center and fuse tag appliqué to right side of fused paper. Trim paper ¹/₄" outside appliqué. Fuse heart appliqué to tag. Punch a hole in point of tag; thread a 4" length of floss through hole and tie to secure.

3. Fuse web to a 6" square of fabric. Use pinking shears to trim ¹/₄" from edges of square.

4. Arrange tag, cookie, and gingerbread man appliqués on fabric square; fuse in place. Center and fuse square to top of box lid.

5. Use pen to write "Cookies for Santa" on tag and to draw designs on box.

6. Referring to *Painting Basics* (pg. 188), use dimensional paint to decorate cookies.

7. Fuse web tape to a 1" x 26" strip of coordinating fabric. Pink long edges of strip; fuse to sides of box lid, overlapping ends.

8. Tie a 1" x 12" strip of coordinating fabric into a bow; glue to front side of lid.

This no-fuss gift will inspire a holly-jolly holiday! Using silk holly leaves makes quick work of the appliquéd letters. Just follow our easy method for fusing the leaves in place, then add a bow and acrylic-jewel "berries."

HOLLY JOY SWEATSHIRT

You will need: silk holly with small leaves, aluminum foil, paper-backed fusible web, ecru sweatshirt, red acrylic jewels, 1"w red satin ribbon, safety pin, and jewel glue.

1. Remove holly leaves from stem.

2. Referring to *Fusing Basics* (pg. 187), follow Foil Method to fuse web to holly leaves.

3. Arrange holly leaves on sweatshirt front to spell out JOY; fuse in place.

4. For berries, follow glue manufacturer's instructions to glue jewels to leaves; allow to dry.

5. Tie ribbon into a bow; use safety pin on wrong side of shirt front to attach bow.

IN ONLY 40 MINUTES!

*A*s cute as a button, our spirited snowman necklace and festive pins are easy to fashion! Make each in only 40 minutes or less. This colorful jewelry is also easy on your pocketbook when made using felt scraps and treasures from your button box.

BUTTON JEWELRY
You will need: scraps of white, gold, blue, red, and green felt; assorted buttons; tracing paper; and craft glue.

For snowman necklace, you will also need: red, brown, and black embroidery floss; black and yellow fine-point markers; and three large white buttons (ours measure $3/4$" dia., 1" dia., and $1^1/8$" dia.) for snowman.

For wreath pin, you will also need: red and green embroidery floss, pinking shears, and a pin back.

For tree pin, you will also need: white embroidery floss and a pin back.

Snowman Necklace
1. Arrange large buttons for snowman on blue felt. Use red embroidery floss to sew buttons for body in place. Referring to *Embroidery Stitches* (pg. 189), use black floss to sew on button for head by working French Knots for eyes. Position buttons for hands on felt and use brown floss to stitch in place. Use long stitches between hands and body for arms.

2. Trace hat, hat trim, and pom-pom patterns (pg. 170) onto tracing paper; cut out. Use patterns to cut pieces from gold and red felt. Arrange hat pieces on blue felt and glue in place; allow to dry. Use markers to draw mouth and nose.

3. Trim blue felt $1/8$" outside edges of snowman.

4. Cut three pieces of embroidery floss the desired length for necklace; place pieces together. Knotting floss between stacks of buttons, thread buttons onto floss. Glue center of necklace to back of snowman head; allow to dry.

5. Place snowman and necklace on white felt piece and glue in place; allow to dry. Trim white felt $1/8$" outside edges of blue felt, using care not to cut floss.

Wreath Pin
1. Trace wreath A and wreath B patterns (pg. 170) onto tracing paper; cut out. Use patterns and pinking shears to cut wreaths from felt.

2. Use embroidery floss to sew buttons to wreath A. Use two colors of embroidery floss to make bow for top of wreath A. Glue bow to wreath; allow to dry.

3. Center and glue wreath A to wreath B; allow to dry.

4. Glue pin back to back of wreath; allow to dry.

Tree Pin
1. Trace tree A, tree B, tree C, and tree trunk patterns (pg. 170) onto tracing paper; cut out. Use patterns to cut tree pieces from felt. Arrange pieces on white felt and glue in place; allow to dry. Work Running Stitch (pg. 189) along edges of tree and trunk.

2. Use embroidery floss to sew buttons to tree as desired. Trim white felt $1/8$"outside edges of tree. Glue tree to red felt; allow to dry. Trim red felt $1/8$" outside edges of white felt.

3. Glue pin back to back of tree; allow to dry.

Spruce up a tasteful and ever-popular gift by tucking a bottle of wine in an easy-to-make wrapper. You can make two bags from one kitchen towel, then complete the cordial look with bells, bows, and wintry flourishes.

WINE BAGS

You will need: one large kitchen towel, thread to match, two 20" lengths of $2^1/_8$"w wired ribbon, floral wire, two 35mm jingle bells, and two sprigs of artificial greenery.

1. With right sides together, fold towel in half lengthwise. Using a $^1/_2$" seam allowance, sew long edges of towel together. Matching short edges, fold towel in half; mark towel along fold. Unfold towel and stitch $^1/_2$" from each side of mark. Cut towel in half along mark.

2. Turn bags right side out. Place a bottle in each bag.

3. Gathering top of each bag around bottle neck, tie in place with wired-ribbon bow. Thread floral wire through knot to secure bell to bow; tuck greenery sprig behind ribbon.

A very special friend will love having a crafty place to record holiday memories. In just minutes, you can create a rustic volume with a wintry touch by gluing frayed fabric shapes and buttons onto a blank journal.

SNOWMAN JOURNAL

You will need: 5" x 7" blank book or journal, tracing paper, scraps of white and orange fabric for snowman, 4³/₄" x 6¹/₄" and 3¹/₂" x 5" torn fabric rectangles, black pen, ¹/₂" x 7" torn fabric strip for scarf, four ³/₈" dia. green buttons, and craft glue.

1. Trace circle A, circle B, circle C, and nose patterns (pg. 173) onto tracing paper; cut out. Use patterns to cut pieces for snowman from fabric; fray edges of circles.

2. Center large rectangle on front of journal and glue in place. Center small rectangle on large rectangle and glue in place. Arrange pieces for snowman on small rectangle and glue in place. Use pen to draw eyes and mouth on face. Knot fabric strip for scarf and glue to snowman.

3. Glue buttons to corners of small rectangle.

*W*hat an impressive gift!
Friends and family will love serving
their cookies in customized style.
In no time, you can prepare these
dazzling plates by decoupaging clear
glass dishes with pretty paper napkins
or Christmas cards.

DECOUPAGED PLATES

For each plate, you will need: clear glass
plate, Christmas card, foam paintbrush,
sponge piece, and decoupage glue.

For cardinal plate, you will also need:
Christmas paper napkin.

For tree plate, you will also need: cream
and metallic gold acrylic paint.

(**Note:** Use plates for dry foods only;
wipe clean with damp cloth.)

1. Cut design from Christmas card front
and trim as desired. Follow glue
manufacturer's instructions to decoupage
card to back of plate.

2. For cardinal plate, use foam brush to
apply a thin coat of decoupage glue to
entire back of plate. Place napkin wrong
side up over glue; smooth in place,
working out air bubbles. Allow to dry to
the touch. Trim edge of napkin even with
edge of plate. Apply a second coat of glue
over napkin.

3. For tree plate, refer to *Painting Basics*
(pg. 188) and use sponge to lightly apply
cream, then metallic gold paint to back of
plate, allowing to dry between colors.

ELF CHALKBOARD
(Continued from page 119)

3. Using patterns, cut head from peach craft foam, hat from green craft foam, and hatband from red craft foam.

4. Glue hatband and bell on hat; glue hat to top of head.

5. Use pen to draw face. Apply blush to cheeks.

6. For hair, cut a 1" length of twine; fray slightly. Glue hair below hat.

7. Glue elf to chalkboard frame.

8. Adhere two 4" lengths of magnetic strip to back of chalkboard.

PILLOW COVER
(Continued from page 19)

of print napkins to front of pillow over red napkin. Concealing pins on the inside, pin edges of napkins together at sides and along top of pillow (Fig. 1).

Fig. 1

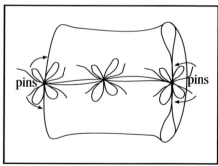

CORDUROY SNOWMAN STOCKING
(Continued from page 25)

6. For hanger, cut a 2¼" x 7" strip of black corduroy. Matching right sides and long edges, sew together; turn right side out. Fold in half and sew ends to inside top edge of stocking.

7. For hat band, tear a 1" x 19" strip of flannel. Tie strip into a knot around hat.

8. Tear a 2" x 18" strip from flannel. Tie into a bow; sew to stocking front.

FESTIVE HOLIDAY MITTENS
(Continued from page 100)

GREEN MITTENS

1. Trace pattern, page 151, onto tracing paper; cut out. Using pattern, cut two snowmen from white felt.

2. Pin one snowman on each mitten. Using green floss, work Blanket Stitch around edge of snowman. Using black floss, work French Knots for eyes and mouth and Stem Stitch for arms. Using orange floss, work Satin Stitch for nose.

3. For snowflakes, sew six buttons to each mitten.

RED MITTENS

1. Trace patterns, page 151, onto tracing paper; cut out. Using patterns, cut trees from green felt and tree trunks from black felt. Overlapping as necessary, pin felt pieces to mittens. Using green floss, work Blanket Stitch around edges of each tree and tree trunk.

2. Use ecru floss to sew buttons to tree and mitten cuff.

MEMORY BOX
(Continued from page 117)

3. Cut a 14" x 18" rectangle from fabric. Center box lid on wrong side of fabric rectangle. Folding in excess fabric at corners, bring fabric edges to inside of lid; glue in place.

4. Cut two 18" lengths of cord. Crossing cords diagonally over box lid, glue ends of each length to opposite corners.

5. Cut a 38" length of cord. Form cord into a diamond shape with points extending over edges of lid; center points of diamond on each side of lid and glue in place. Cut off any excess cord. Glue a button over each point of cord.

6. Working from top side of lid, use push pin to make a hole at each side of each cord intersection. Use nylon thread to stitch cord to lid, pulling thread taut and tying into a knot on wrong side of lid. Place a dot of glue over each knot.

CHRISTMAS KITCHEN ANGEL
(Continued from page 21)

3. For hair, cut two 24" lengths of floss. Placing lengths together, thread tapestry needle; knot ½" from end. Beginning at eye level on head seam, take a small stitch. Knot floss at end of stitch and cut ½" from knot. Repeat along seam to opposite side of head.

4. For body, tear an 11" x 12" rectangle from muslin. Center and pin message pattern to right half of rectangle. Work Running Stitch for words, stems, and leaves of flowers. Work Lazy Daisy Stitch for center flower petals and French Knots for flower center. Sew a button to top of each remaining stem.

5. Matching wrong sides, fold body in half. Insert head between layers at top of body; pin in place. Leaving an opening for stuffing, use gold floss to sew ½" from raw edges. Stuff body with fiberfill; sew opening closed. Sew a button below neck. Tie a 10" length of red floss into a bow around button; tie a knot at end of each streamer.

6. For arms, center 12" twig on back of angel; glue in place. Glue a small piece of cedar and bird to one arm.

7. For wings, glue cedar branches to back of angel above arms.

8. For legs, insert 2" of remaining twigs between stitches at bottom of body; glue in place.

9. For halo, cut a 6" length of twine; tie ends together, forming a loop. Glue halo to back of head.

10. For hanger, thread needle with a 4" length of floss. Take a stitch on back of head; tie ends of floss into a knot.

HOMESPUN ANGEL
(Continued from page 59)

3. Draw face on back of spoon. Use red pencil to color cheeks.

4. Gather dress around spoon handle; secure with rubber band. Adjust gathers evenly. For apron, fold 2¹/₂" of one doily to right side. Folding sides of doily to wrong side, position over gathers of dress; glue in place. Cut a 26" length of each color ribbon. Tie ribbons together in a bow around neck of angel. Glue 1" button over knot of bow.

5. For wings, tie a length of string tightly around center of remaining doily; adjust gathers evenly. Glue wings to back of angel.

6. Cut a 9" length of doll hair and a 3¹/₂" length of ecru ribbon. Tie ribbon in a knot around center of hair length; fluff hair slightly. Glue hair to top of angel head.

7. Remove three leaves from holly sprig. Glue one leaf over knot of hair ribbon and two leaves to front of dress.

HOLLY TREE SKIRT
(Continued from page 28)

2. Referring to *Cutting a Fabric Circle*, page 191, cut a 40" dia. circle from corduroy. Repeat to cut a 7" dia. circle from center of large circle. For opening, cut through one layer of fabric from outer to inner edge. Turn all raw edges ¹/₂" to wrong side; press. Clip curves.

3. Fuse web tape to wrong side of turned edges of tree skirt. Remove paper backing and fuse hems in place.

4. Using three strands of floss, work Running Stitch, page 189, to sew leaves to tree skirt.

5. Using yo-yo patterns, cut nineteen of each size circle from green fabrics. Turn raw edge of each circle ¹/₈" to wrong side. Using a double strand of thread, hand

baste along turned edge. Pull threads to tightly gather circle; knot thread and trim ends. Flatten circle. Sew yo-yos to tree skirt.

PAINTBRUSH SANTAS
(Continued from page 61)

3. Use three strands of floss to work Straight Stitch, page 189, for eyelashes and mouth.

4. For mustache, cut an ¹/₈" dia. bundle of bristles from back of paintbrush. Knot thread around center of bundle; clip thread ends close to mustache. Glue mustache to head. Glue head to paintbrush.

5. For hat, use pinking shears to cut a 6" square from red felt. For hat trim, cut two ³/₄" x 6" strips of lamb's wool; glue to two edges of hat as shown in Fig. 1.

Fig. 1

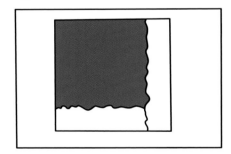

6. Position paintbrush diagonally over wrong side of hat. Wrap hat around paintbrush; glue in place.

7. Glue a pom-pom to top of hat.

FELT CANVAS TOTE BAG
(Continued from page 107)

6. Cut a 19" length of rickrack; hand sew to edge of gingerbread boy. For bow tie, cut a 6" length of red ribbon. Fold ribbon into a bow; wrap red floss around center to secure. Glue bow to gingerbread boy.

7. Sew buttons on front of each figure.

8. Measure around top of bag; add 1". Use pinking shears to cut a strip of fabric 1¹/₄" by the determined measurement; cut a length of ¹/₂"w green ribbon the determined measurement. Center web tape on wrong side of fabric strip; fuse in place. Overlapping ends ¹/₂", fuse fabric strip to top of bag. Glue ribbon length along center of fabric strip. Center buttons on ribbon along front of bag; sew in place.

9. Use pinking shears to cut two ¹/₂" x 7" strips of fabric. Tie each strip into a bow. Cut a 19" length of ¹/₈"w ribbon. Leaving a 2" tail at each end, glue ribbon to center front of bag, 1¹/₄" from each edge.

10. Spacing 1" apart, glue Santas and gingerbread boy along ribbon. Glue fabric bows between figures.

CHRISTMAS CARD WALL HANGING
(Continued from page 29)

5. For hanging sleeve, cut 4" x 35" pieces from fabric and fusible interfacing; fuse together. Press edges ¹/₂" to wrong side. Fuse a length of web tape along top and bottom edges of hanging sleeve. Position hanging sleeve on wrong side of wall hanging ¹/₄" below top edge; fuse in place.

6. Using pattern, page 186, make two gingerbread boy appliqués from tan fabric. Cut two 5¹/₂" x 7" pieces from felt. Center one gingerbread boy on each felt piece; fuse in place. Use pinking shears to trim felt ¹/₄" outside edges of gingerbread boys.

7. Using black floss, work Running Stitch to outline gingerbread boys, French Knots for eyes, and Stem Stitch for mouth. Punch two holes from red fabric scrap for cheeks for each gingerbread boy; glue in place.

8. Tear two ¹/₂" x 6" strips from fabric scraps; tie each into a bow. Glue one bow on each gingerbread boy.

9. Paint wooden heart buttons red; allow to dry. Use red embroidery floss to sew heart buttons and ³/₄" dia. buttons to gingerbread boys; glue to wall hanging.

10. Cut 5" x 11" rectangles from red fabric and fusible web; fuse together; do not remove paper backing. With stencils reversed, use pencil to draw around letters on paper side of fused rectangle; cut out. Position letters on background; fuse in place.

11. Leaving 5" streamers on each end, tie ribbon to buttons. Attach cards to ribbon with clothespins. Insert dowel through hanging sleeve.

"NO PEEKIN'" DOOR HANGER
(Continued from page 17)

Fig. 2

6. Spacing loops ¹/₂" apart and leaving floss slack between loops (Fig. 3), repeat Step 5 to add each remaining bell to pillow. Bring needle to back of pillow and secure floss.

Fig. 3

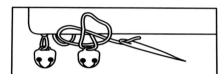

SNOW FRIENDS BASKET
(Continued from page 104)

5. For stocking hat, cut 5" from ribbing end of one red sock. Fold finished edge of ribbing 1" to right side. Tie jute into a bow around middle of ribbing. Glue hat to one head.

6. For nightcap, use compass to draw a 6" dia. circle pattern on tracing paper. Cut foot part of red sock open and lay flat. Using circle pattern, cut cap from sock piece; glue lace trim around edge. Baste around circle ¹/₂" inside edge. Pull thread ends to loosely gather cap; knot thread ends to secure. Lightly stuff cap with fiberfill. Glue cap to remaining head.

7. Matching ends of each pair of arms at ends of basket and placing arms along sides of basket, glue arms in place. Glue heads to top edge of basket where arms join.

8. For each scarf, tear a 1¹/₄" x 19" strip of fabric. Loosely tie strip around base of each head.

PATTERNS

SNOWMAN SWEATSHIRT

Christmas is Cool!

SMILE

NOSE

Everyone needs elves!

HATBAND

HAT

ELF CHALKBOARD

HEAD

KISS ME!!

MISTLETOE HAT

LARGE LEAVES

SMALL LEAVES

FESTIVE HOLIDAY MITTENS

SNOWMAN

TREE

TREE
TRUNK

PATTERNS (continued)

GARDEN STONE SANTA

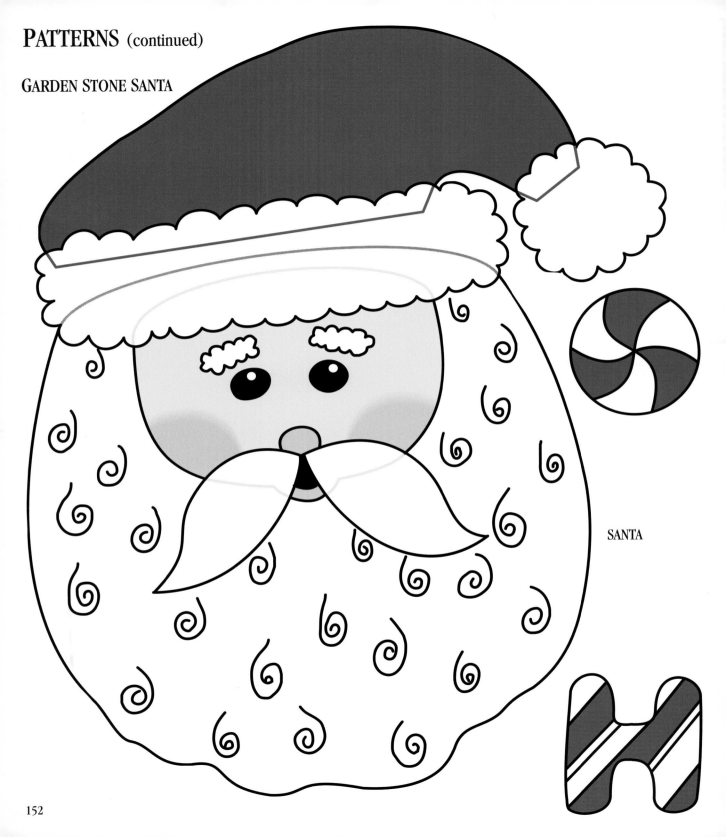

SANTA

MITTEN ORNAMENTS
AND
FESTIVE WOOL
BLANKET

FLOWER

FLOWER
CENTER

MITTEN

MITTEN CUFF

HEAD

CHRISTMAS KITCHEN ANGEL

153

PATTERNS (continued)

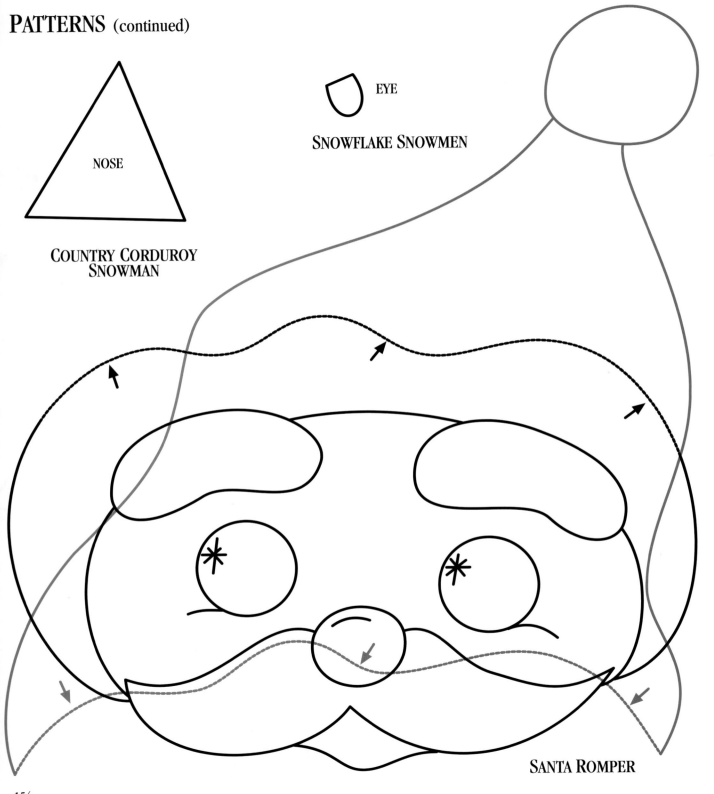

NOSE

EYE

SNOWFLAKE SNOWMEN

COUNTRY CORDUROY
SNOWMAN

SANTA ROMPER

LEAF C

HOLLY TREE SKIRT

LARGE YO-YO

SMALL YO-YO

LEAF D

LEAF A

LEAF B

ETCHED NATIVITY GLOBE

155

PATTERNS (continued)

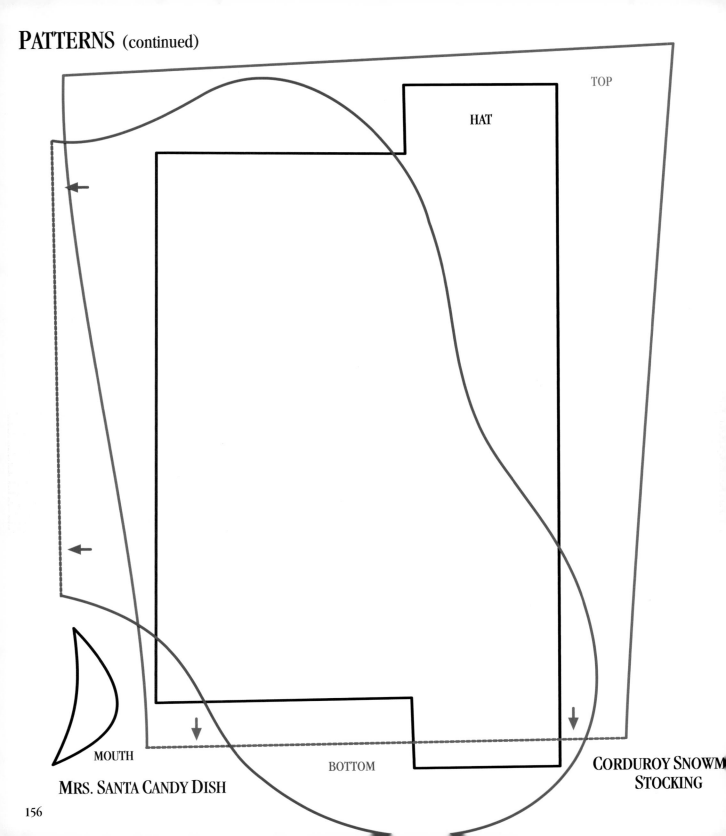

TOP

HAT

MOUTH

BOTTOM

MRS. SANTA CANDY DISH

CORDUROY SNOWM
STOCKING

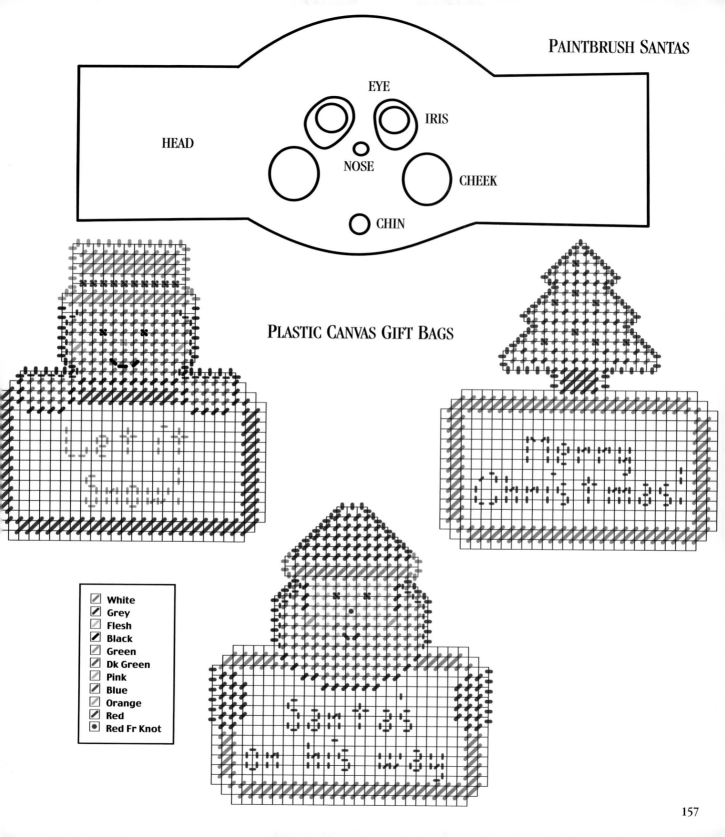

PAINTBRUSH SANTAS

HEAD

EYE

IRIS

NOSE

CHEEK

CHIN

PLASTIC CANVAS GIFT BAGS

White
Grey
Flesh
Black
Green
Dk Green
Pink
Blue
Orange
Red
Red Fr Knot

157

PATTERNS (continued)

FABRIC-COVERED BASKET

BERRY

LEAF

POM-POM

BEARD

GINGERBREAD BOY

MUSTACHE

CUFF

SANTA

FACE

**JOLLY FELT
WREATH
AND
FUN FELT CANVAS
TOTE BAG**

BOOTS

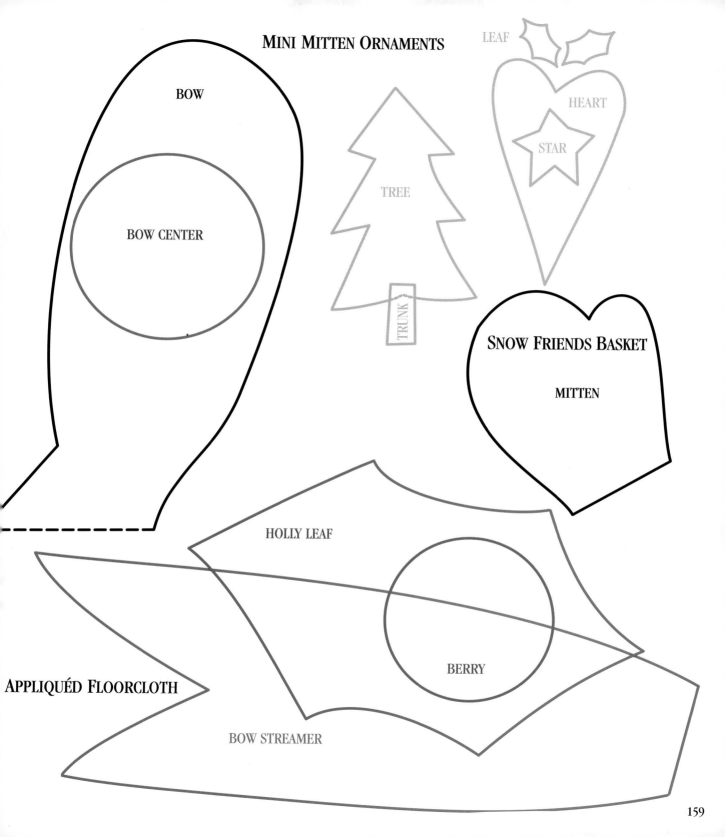

MINI MITTEN ORNAMENTS

BOW

BOW CENTER

LEAF

HEART

STAR

TREE

TRUNK

SNOW FRIENDS BASKET

MITTEN

HOLLY LEAF

BERRY

APPLIQUÉD FLOORCLOTH

BOW STREAMER

PATTERNS (continued)

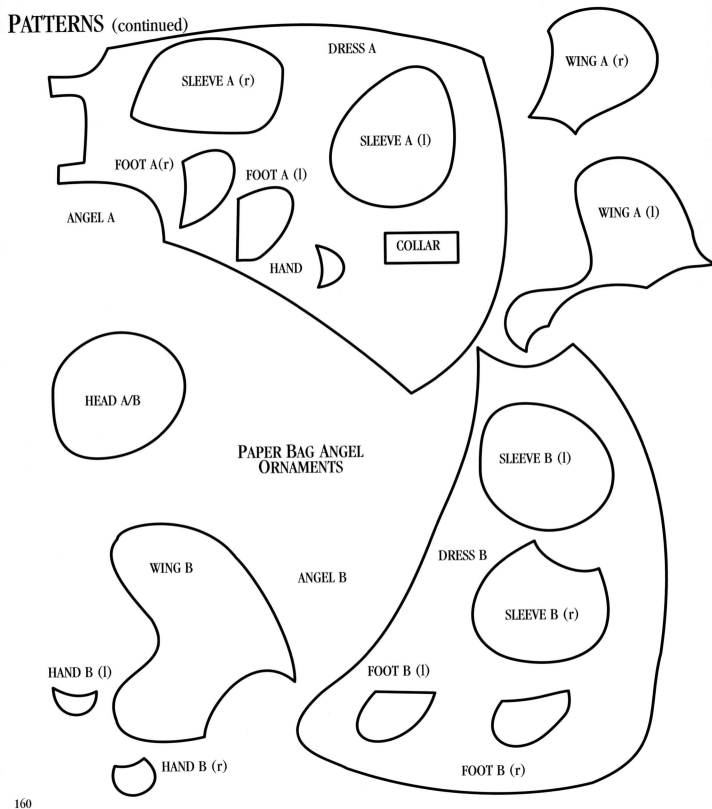

DRESS A

SLEEVE A (r)

WING A (r)

SLEEVE A (l)

FOOT A(r)

FOOT A (l)

WING A (l)

ANGEL A

COLLAR

HAND

HEAD A/B

PAPER BAG ANGEL
ORNAMENTS

SLEEVE B (l)

WING B

ANGEL B

DRESS B

SLEEVE B (r)

HAND B (l)

FOOT B (l)

HAND B (r)

FOOT B (r)

SHIRT

HAT

COLLAR

ELF ORNAMENT

HAND

HEAD

FOOT

HEART

FLEECE PLACE MATS

STAR

BULB

CIRCLE

SOCKET

HANDMADE
CHRISTMAS CARDS

PATTERNS (continued)

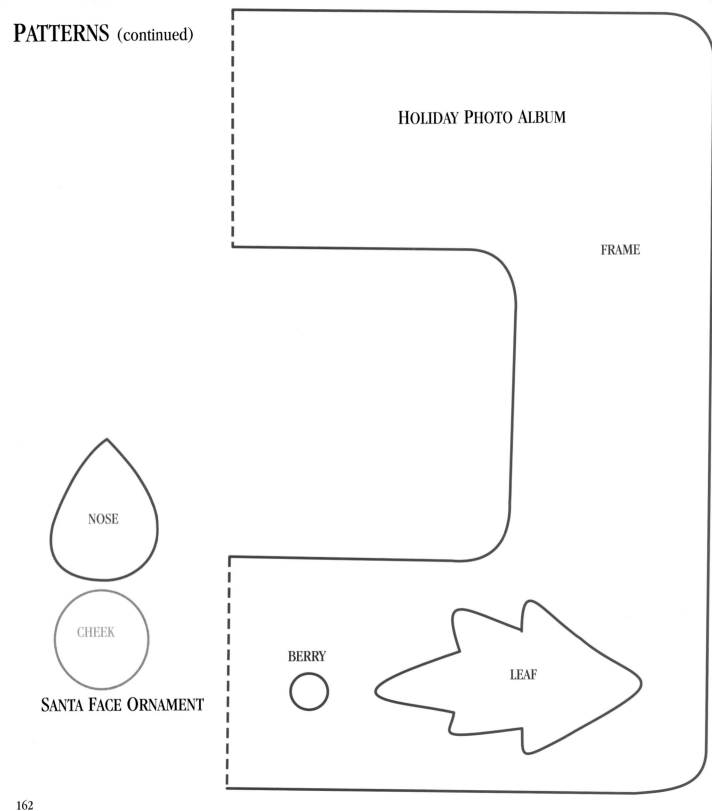

HOLIDAY PHOTO ALBUM

FRAME

NOSE

CHEEK

SANTA FACE ORNAMENT

BERRY

LEAF

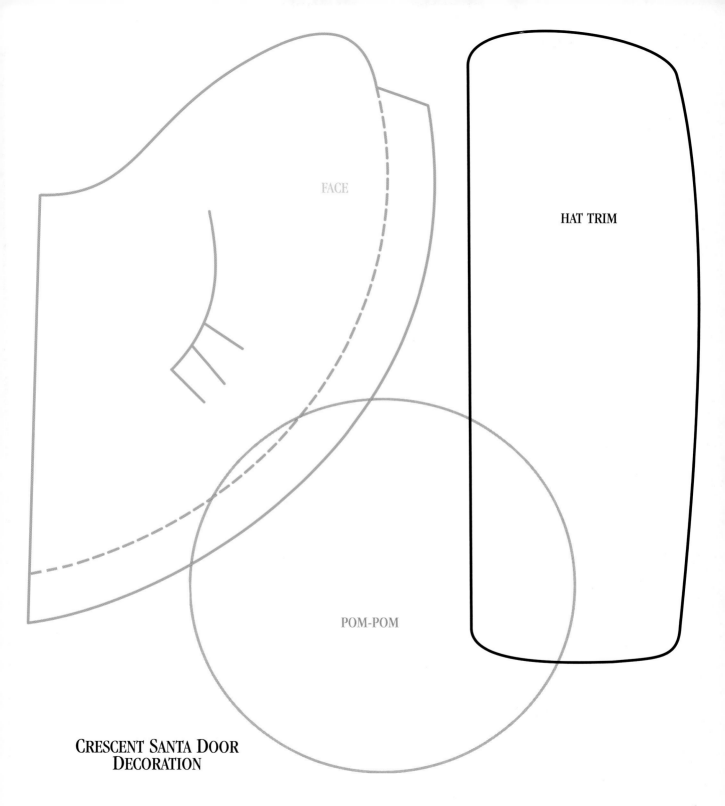

FACE

HAT TRIM

POM-POM

**CRESCENT SANTA DOOR
DECORATION**

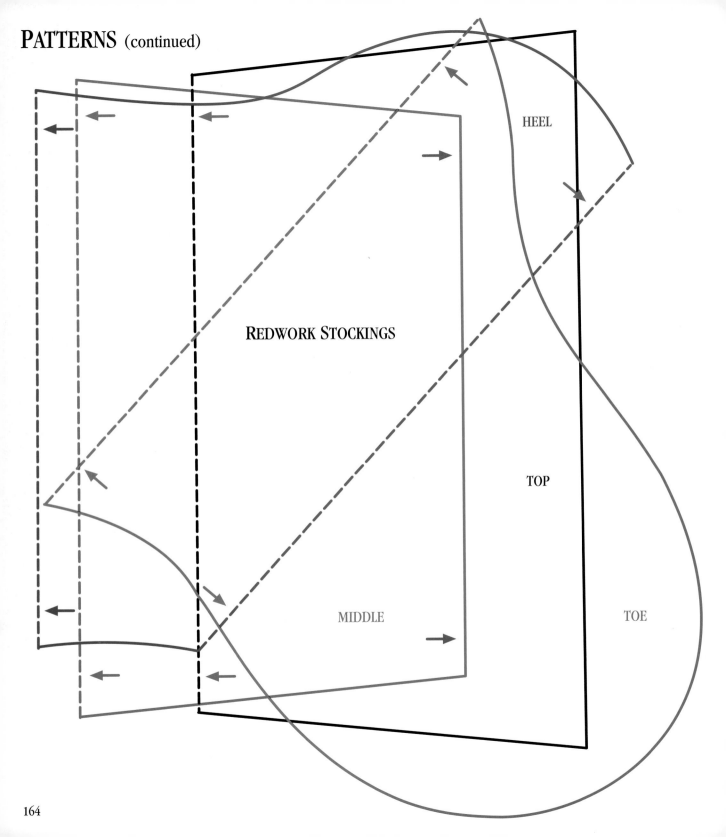

REDWORK STOCKINGS

HEEL

TOP

TOE

MIDDLE

CHRISTMAS BABY BIBS

NECK OPENING

MERRY CHRISTMAS

REDWORK STOCKINGS
(continued)

PATTERNS (continued)

LARGE HEART

SMALL HEART

LEAVES

HEART POCKET ORNAMENT

LEAF

N o Peekin'

"NO PEEKIN'" DOOR HANGER

It's Christmas!

time to trim the tree,
Wrap the Gifts,
Bake the Cookies,
And spend time
With Friends

PATTERNS (continued)

TREE

KIDS' PHOTO BOOKS

CHEEK

HEART

SNOWMAN

GINGERBREAD MAN

RUSTIC HOLIDAY WREATH

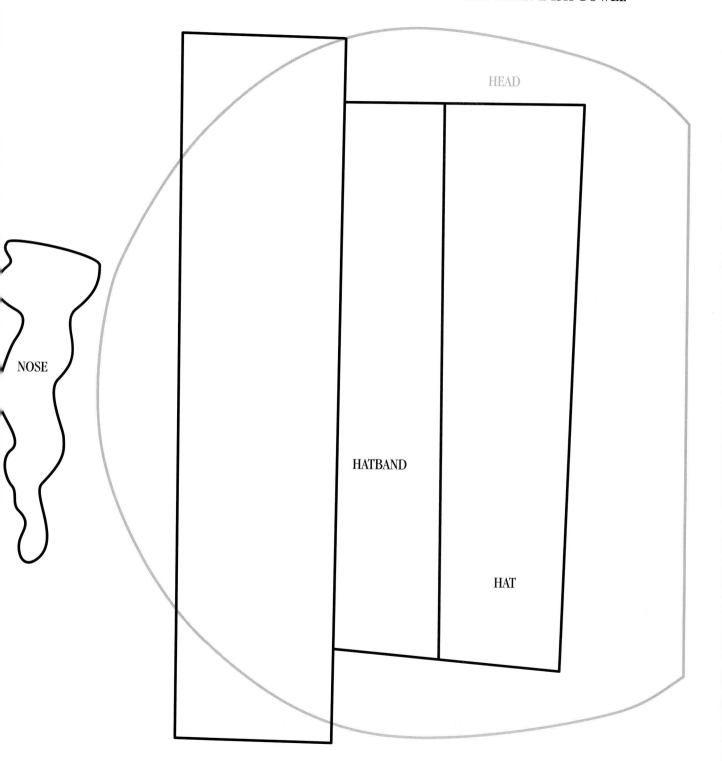

NOSE

HEAD

HATBAND

HAT

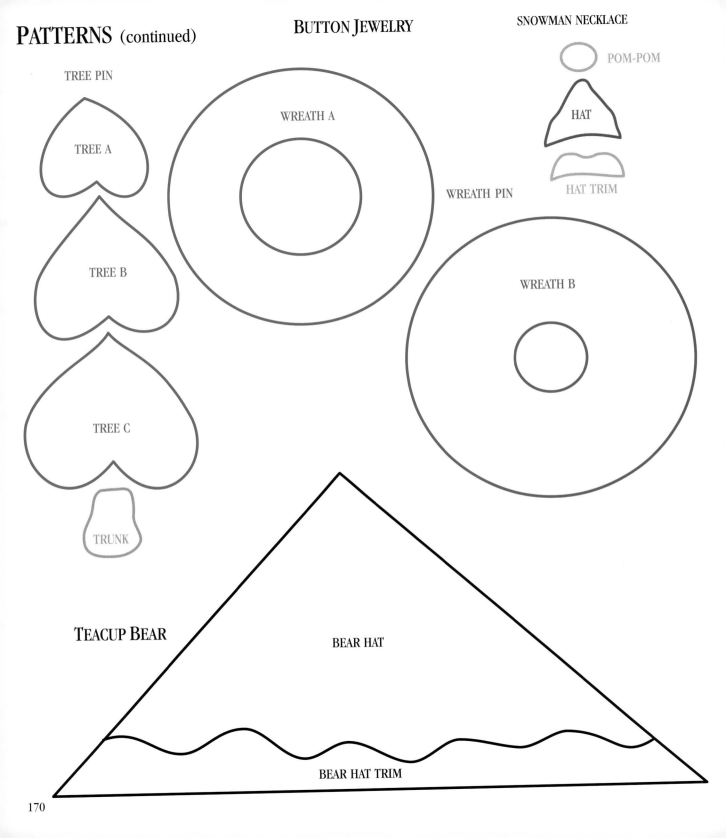

PATTERNS (continued)

BUTTON JEWELRY

SNOWMAN NECKLACE

POM-POM

HAT

HAT TRIM

TREE PIN

TREE A

TREE B

TREE C

TRUNK

WREATH A

WREATH PIN

WREATH B

TEACUP BEAR

BEAR HAT

BEAR HAT TRIM

170

REINDEER ORNAMENT

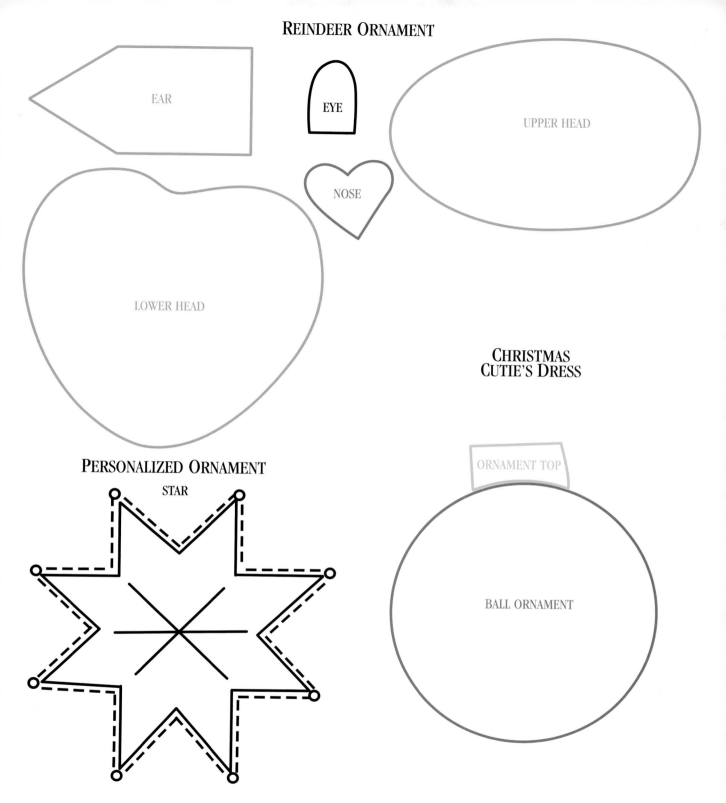

EAR

EYE

UPPER HEAD

NOSE

LOWER HEAD

CHRISTMAS CUTIE'S DRESS

PERSONALIZED ORNAMENT

STAR

ORNAMENT TOP

BALL ORNAMENT

PATTERNS (continued)

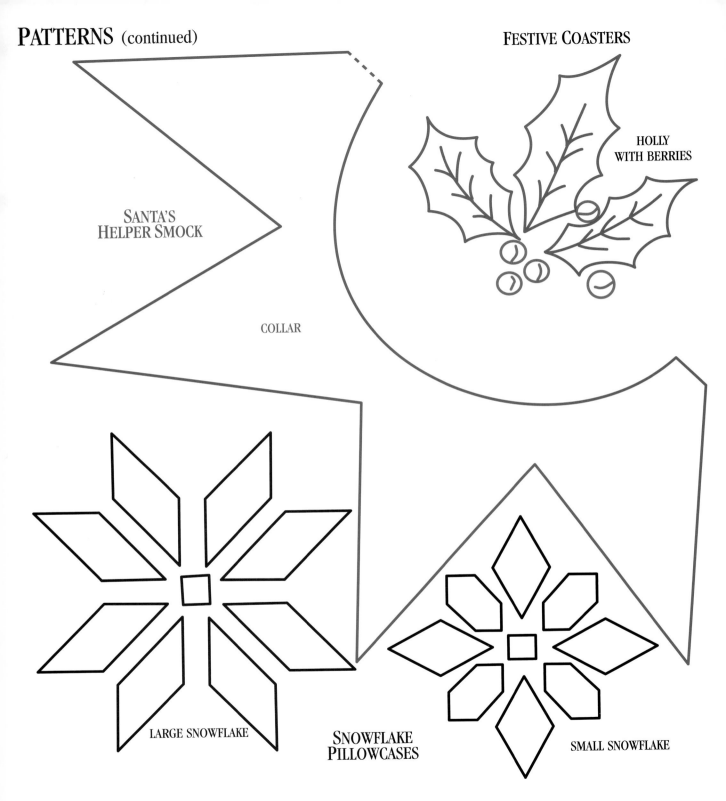

FESTIVE COASTERS

HOLLY
WITH BERRIES

SANTA'S
HELPER SMOCK

COLLAR

LARGE SNOWFLAKE

SNOWFLAKE
PILLOWCASES

SMALL SNOWFLAKE

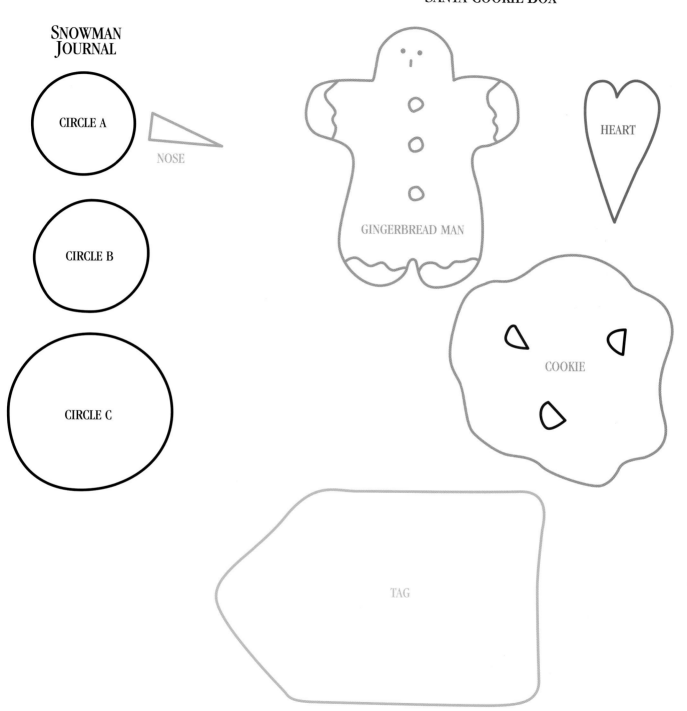

SNOWMAN
JOURNAL

CIRCLE A

NOSE

CIRCLE B

CIRCLE C

GINGERBREAD MAN MINI TOTE
SANTA COOKIE BOX

GINGERBREAD MAN

HEART

COOKIE

TAG

PATTERNS (continued)

SNOWMEN SWEATSHIRT
CHEERY GIFT BAGS

HOLIDAY BIRDHOUSE

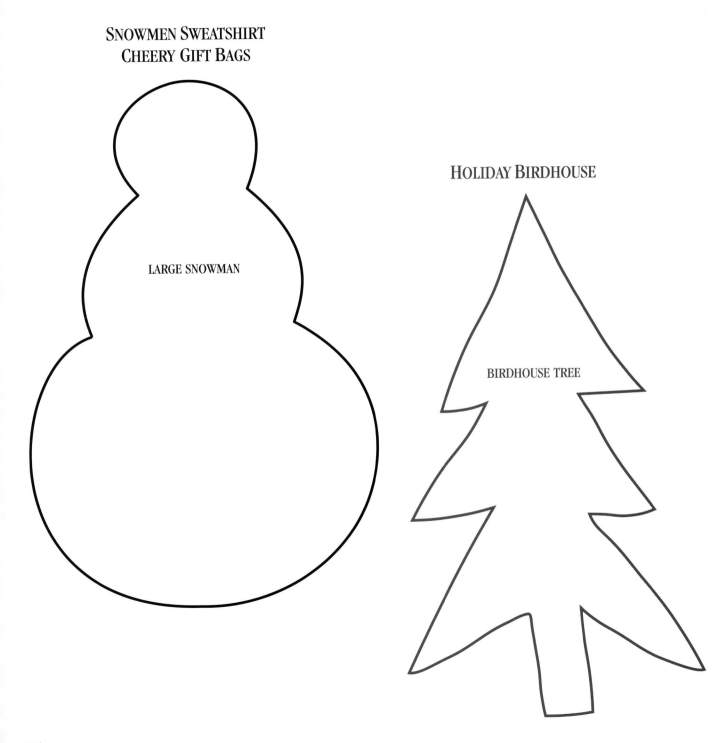

LARGE SNOWMAN

BIRDHOUSE TREE

FROSTY SWEATSHIRT
SNOWMAN WREATH

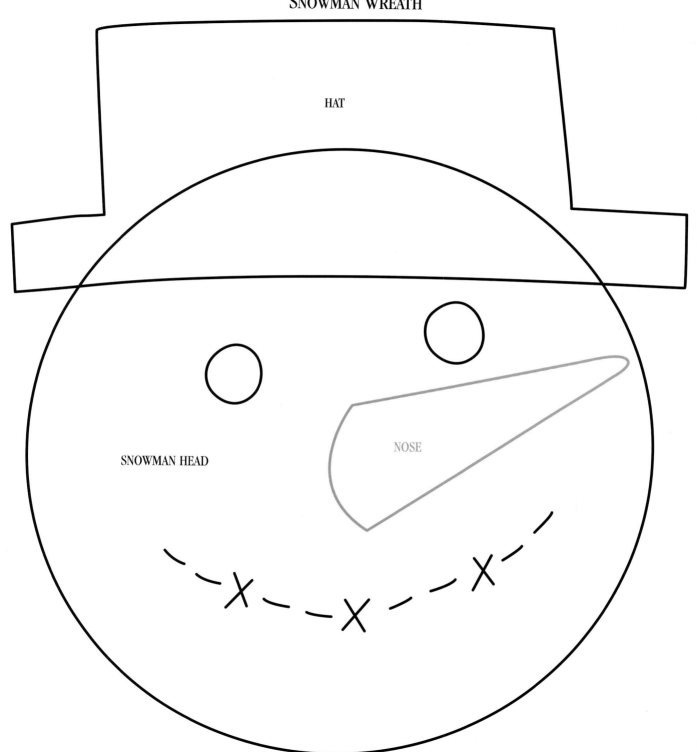

HAT

SNOWMAN HEAD

NOSE

PATTERNS (continued)

HEART CHARM STOCKING

HURRICANE SNOWMAN FATHER CHRISTMAS

MITTEN

RIBBON TREE

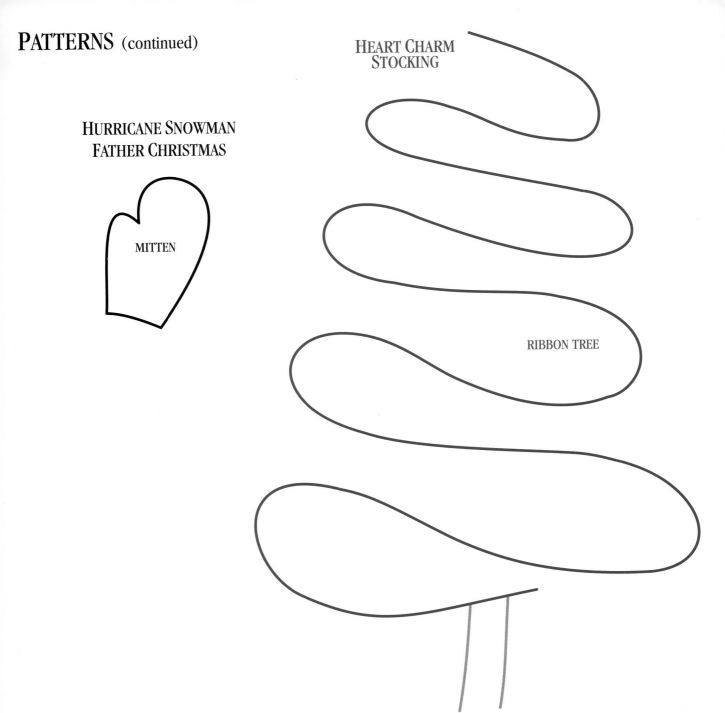

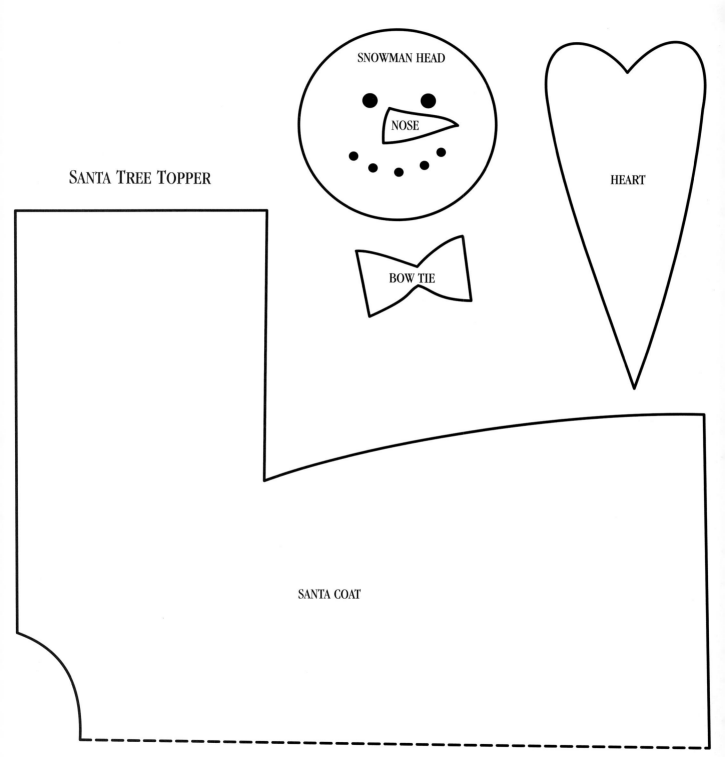

SNOWMAN GARLAND

SNOWMAN HEAD

NOSE

HEART

SANTA TREE TOPPER

BOW TIE

SANTA COAT

PATTERNS (continued)

BIRD-IN-HAND SNOWMAN

BIRD

HAT

BUTTON ANGEL

LARGE ANGEL BODY

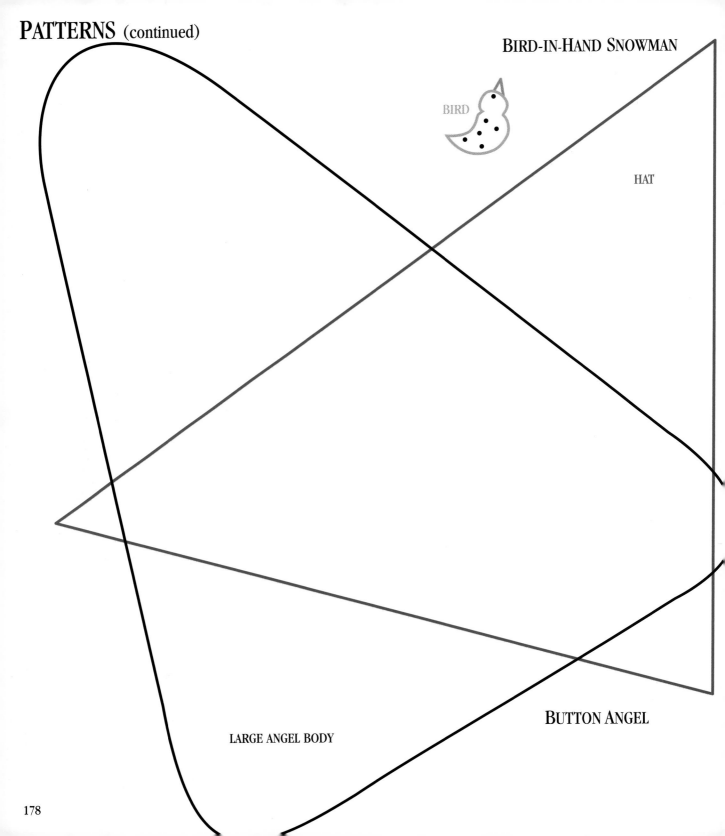

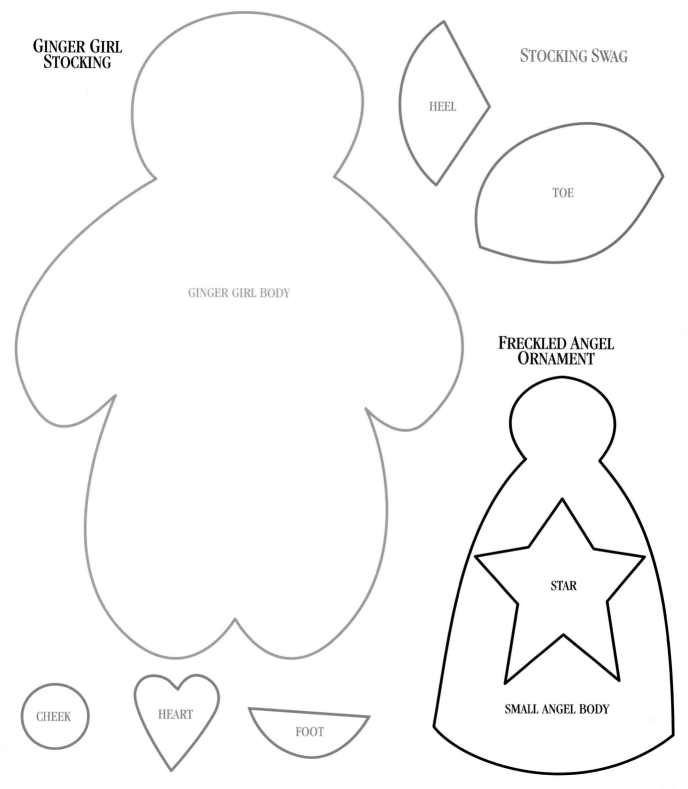

GINGER GIRL
STOCKING

STOCKING SWAG

HEEL

TOE

GINGER GIRL BODY

FRECKLED ANGEL
ORNAMENT

STAR

SMALL ANGEL BODY

CHEEK

HEART

FOOT

179

PATTERNS (continued)

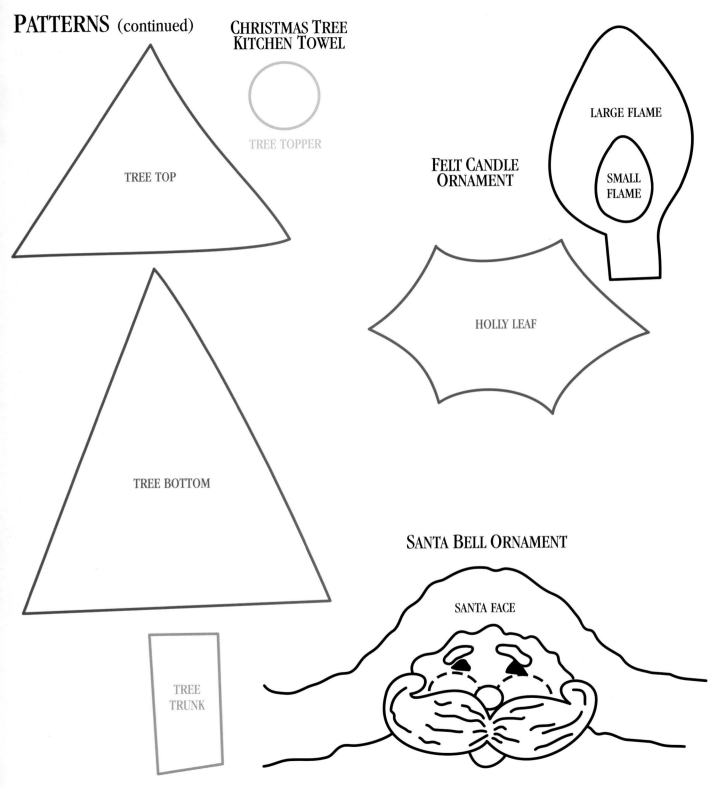

CHRISTMAS TREE
KITCHEN TOWEL

TREE TOPPER

TREE TOP

FELT CANDLE
ORNAMENT

LARGE FLAME

SMALL
FLAME

HOLLY LEAF

TREE BOTTOM

SANTA BELL ORNAMENT

SANTA FACE

TREE
TRUNK

YULETIDE BANNER

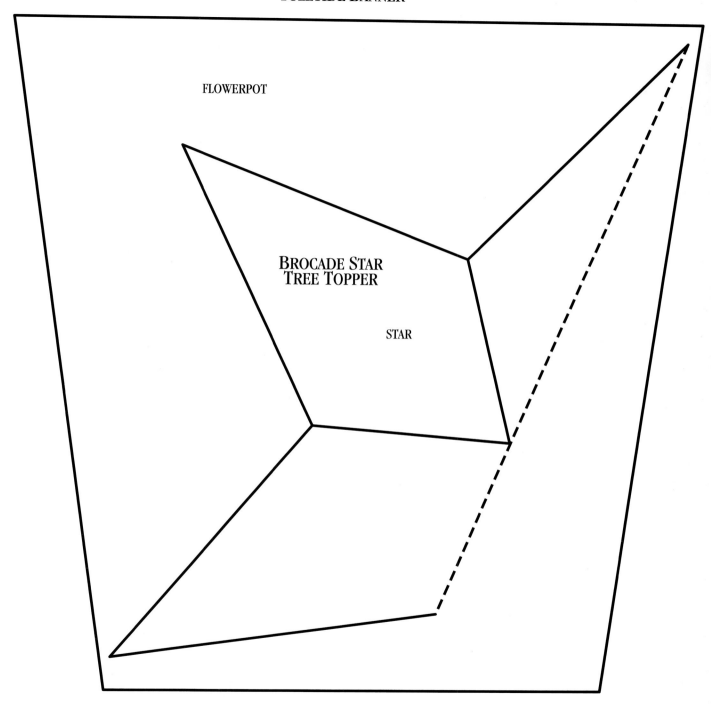

FLOWERPOT

BROCADE STAR
TREE TOPPER

STAR

PATTERNS (continued)

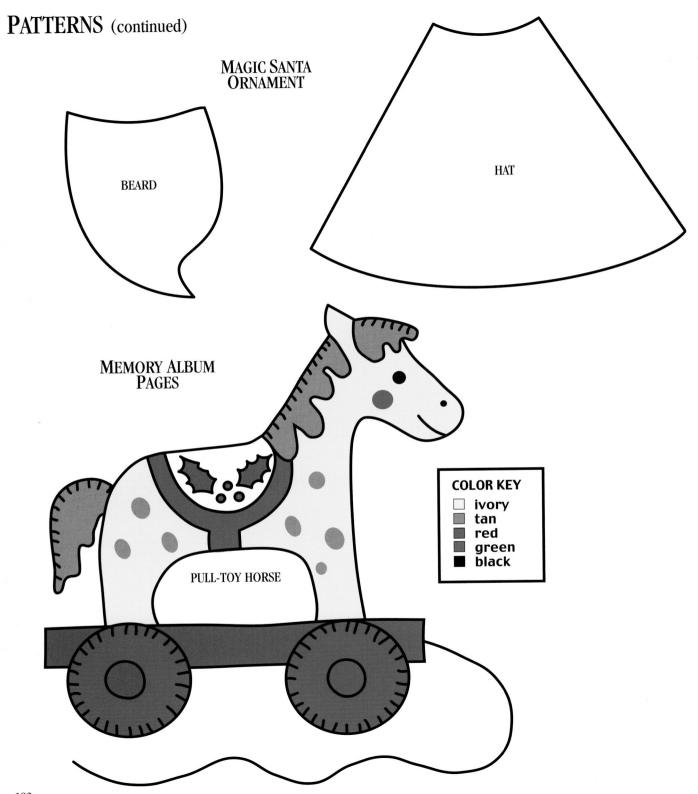

MAGIC SANTA
ORNAMENT

BEARD

HAT

MEMORY ALBUM
PAGES

PULL-TOY HORSE

COLOR KEY

- ivory
- tan
- red
- green
- ■ black

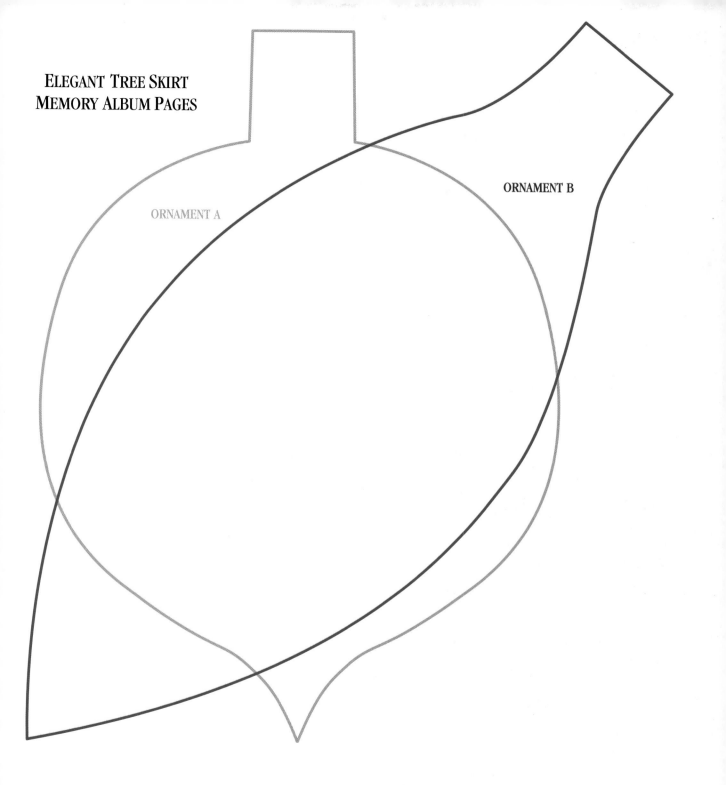

ELEGANT TREE SKIRT
MEMORY ALBUM PAGES

ORNAMENT A

ORNAMENT B

PATTERNS (continued)

FILIGREE ORNAMENTS

FILIGREE ORNAMENT A

GINGERBREAD GIRL ORNAMENT

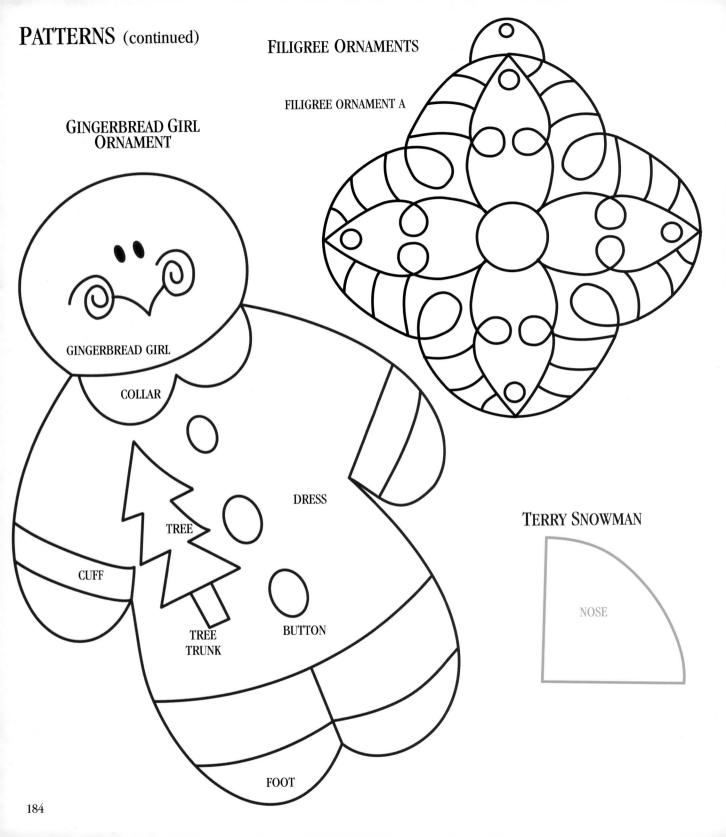

GINGERBREAD GIRL

COLLAR

DRESS

TREE

CUFF

TREE TRUNK

BUTTON

FOOT

TERRY SNOWMAN

NOSE

FILIGREE ORNAMENTS
(continued)

FILIGREE ORNAMENT B

FILIGREE ORNAMENT C

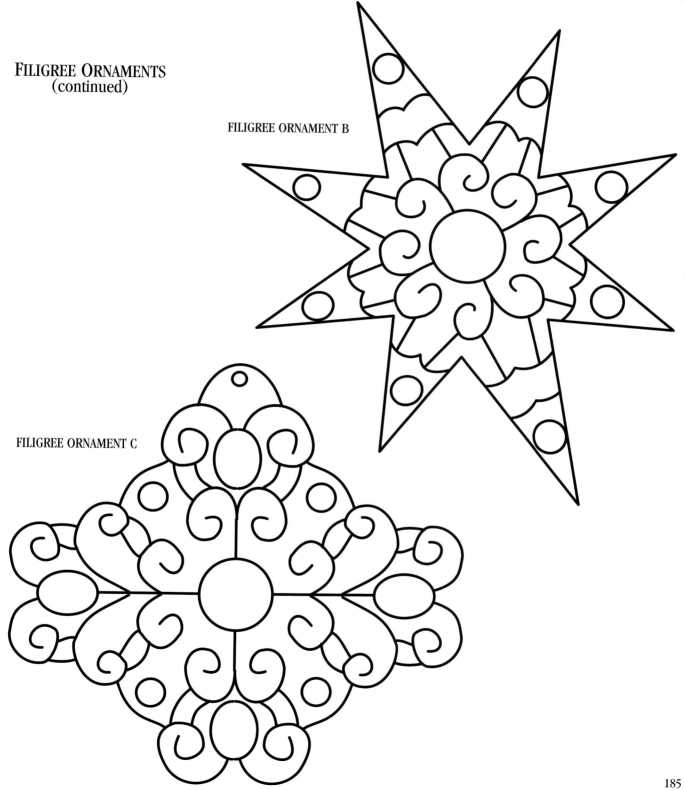

PATTERNS (continued)

CHRISTMAS CARD
WALL HANGING

GINGERBREAD BOY

GENERAL INSTRUCTIONS

ADHESIVES

When using any adhesive, carefully follow the manufacturer's instructions.

White craft glue: Recommended for paper. Dry flat.

Tacky craft glue: Recommended for paper, fabric, floral, or wood. Dry flat or secure items with clothespins or straight pins until glue is dry.

Fabric glue: Recommended for fabric or paper. Dry flat or secure items with clothespins or straight pins until glue is dry.

Decoupage glue: Recommended for decoupaging fabric or paper to a surface such as wood or glass. Use purchased decoupage glue or mix one part craft glue with one part water.

Hot or low-temperature glue gun: Recommended for floral, paper, fabric, or wood. Hold in place until set. A low-temperature glue gun is safer than a hot glue gun, but the bond made with the glue is not as strong.

MAKING PATTERNS

When patterns are stacked or overlapped, place tracing paper over pattern and follow a single colored line to trace pattern. Repeat to trace each pattern separately onto tracing paper.

For a more durable pattern, use translucent vinyl template material instead of tracing paper.

Half-patterns: Fold tracing paper in half. Place fold along dashed line and trace pattern half; turn folded paper over and draw over traced lines on remaining side. Unfold pattern; cut out.

Two-part patterns: Trace one part of pattern onto tracing paper. Match dotted line and arrows of traced part with dotted line and arrows of second part in book

Transferring a pattern: Make a tracing paper pattern. Position pattern on project. Place transfer paper coated side down between pattern and project. Use a stylus to trace over lines of patterns.

FUSING BASICS

(**Note:** To protect your ironing board, cover with muslin. Web material that sticks to iron may be removed with hot iron cleaner, available at fabric and craft stores.)

Using fusible web: Place web side of paper-backed fusible web on wrong side of fabric. Follow manufacturer's instructions to fuse web to fabric. Remove paper backing. Position fused fabric web side down on project and press with heated iron for ten seconds. Repeat, lifting and repositioning iron until all fabric is fused.

Making fusible fabric appliqués: (**Note:** To prevent darker fabrics from showing through, white or light-colored fabrics may need to be lined with fusible interfacing before being fused.)

Trace appliqué pattern onto paper side of web. When making more than one appliqué, leave at least 1" between shapes. Cutting $1/2$" outside drawn shape, cut out web shape. Fuse to wrong side of fabric. Cut out shape along drawn lines. Remove paper backing. If pattern is a half-pattern or to make a reversed appliqué, make a tracincg paper pattern (turn traced pattern over for reversed appliqué) and follow instructions using traced pattern.

Foil method: When applying fusible web to items that are narrow or openwork items (lace, doilies, etc.), place a piece of foil shiny side up under items to prevent web from sticking to ironing board. Place item wrong side up on foil. Place web paper side up over item; press. Peel item from foil; trim excess web. Remove paper backing and fuse to project.

STITCHING APPLIQUÉS

Place paper or stabilizer on wrong side of background fabric under fused or basted appliqué. Unless otherwise indicated in project instructions, use clear nylon thread and a narrow zigzag stitch.

Position project under presser foot so that most of stitching will be on appliqué. Take a stitch in fabric and bring bobbin thread to top. Hold both threads toward you and sew over them for several stitches to secure; clip threads. Stitch over all exposed raw edges of appliqué(s) and along detail lines as indicated in instructions.

When stitching is complete, remove stabilizer. Clip threads close to stitching.

General Instructions (continued)

Painting Basics

Painting with a sponge shape: Use a pen to draw around pattern on a dry compressed craft sponge; cut out shape. Dampen sponge shape to expand. Pour a small amount of paint onto a paper plate. Dip one side of sponge shape into paint and remove excess on a paper towel. Lightly press sponge shape on project, then carefully lift. Reapplying paint to sponge shape as necessary, repeat to paint additional shapes on project.

Stenciling: For stencil, cut a piece of template material at least 1" larger on all sides than pattern. Place template material directly over pattern in book. Use a pen to trace pattern onto template material. Place template material on cutting mat and use craft knife to cut out stencil segments, making sure edges are smooth.

Pour a small amount of paint onto a paper plate. Hold or tape (using removable tape) stencil in place on project. Dip a stencil brush or sponge piece in paint and remove excess on a paper towel. Brush or sponge should be almost dry to produce good results. Beginning at edge of cut-out area, apply paint in a stamping motion over stencil. Carefully remove stencil from project. To stencil a design in reverse, clean stencil and turn stencil over.

Sealing: If an item will be handled frequently or used outdoors, we recommend sealing the item with clear acrylic sealer. Sealers are available in spray or brush-on form in several finishes. Follow manufacturer's instructions to apply sealer.

Painting with dimensional paint: Turn bottle upside down to fill tip before each use. While painting, clean tip often with a paper towel. If tip becomes clogged, insert a straight pin into opening to unclog.

To paint, touch tip to project. Squeezing and moving bottle steadily, apply paint to project, being careful not to flatten paint line. If securing an appliqué, center line of paint to cover raw edge of appliqué. If painting detail lines, center line of paint over transferred line on project or freehand details as desired.

To correct a mistake, use a paring knife to gently scrape excess paint from project before it dries. Carefully remove stain with non-acetone nail polish remover on a cotton swab. A mistake may also be camouflaged by incorporating it into the design.

Dry Brush

Do not dip brush in water. Dip a stipple brush or an old paintbrush in paint; wipe most of the paint off onto a dry paper towel. Using tips of bristles, lightly brush over the surface of the project; decrease pressure on the brush as you move outward. Repeat until desired effect is achieved.

Covering a Lampshade

1. To make pattern, find seamline of lampshade. If shade does not have a seamline, draw a vertical line from top edge to bottom edge of shade.

2. Center tissue paper edge on shade seamline; tape in place. Wrap paper around shade extending one inch past seamline; tape to secure (Fig. 1).

Fig. 1

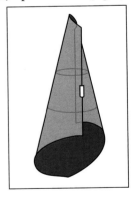

3. Trace along top and bottom edges of shade. Draw a vertical line from top edge to bottom edge of shade 1" past seamline. Remove paper; cut along drawn lines.

EMBROIDERY STITCHES

Preparing floss: If using embroidery floss for a project that will be laundered, soak floss in a mixture of one cup water and one tablespoon vinegar for a few minutes and allow to dry before using to prevent colors from bleeding or fading.

Backstitch: Referring to Fig. 1, come up at 1 and go down at 2; bring up at 3 and pull through. For next stitch, insert needle at 1; bring up at 4 and pull through.
Fig. 1

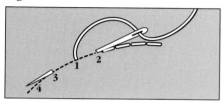

Blanket Stitch: Referring to Fig. 2, bring needle up at 1. Keeping thread below point of needle, go down at 2 and come up at 3. Continue working as shown in Fig. 3.

Fig. 2   **Fig. 3**

Couching Stitch: Thread first needle with desired number of strands of floss to be couched. Thread a second needle with stitching floss. Bring first needle up through fabric. Using second needle, bring needle up at 1 and down at 2 to secure floss (Fig. 4). Repeat to secure floss along desired line.
Fig. 4

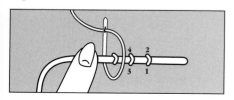

Cross Stitch: Referring to Fig. 5, bring needle up at 1; go down at 2. Bring needle up at 3; go down at 4. Repeat for each stitch.
Fig. 5

French Knot: Referring to Fig. 6, bring needle up at 1. Wrap floss once around needle and insert needle at 2, holding end of floss with non-stitching fingers. Tighten knot, then pull needle through fabric, holding floss until it must be released. For a larger knot, use more strands; wrap only once.
Fig. 6

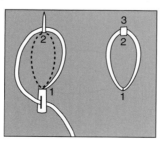

Lazy Daisy Stitch: Referring to Fig. 7, come up at 1 and make a loop with the thread. Go back down at 1 and come up at 2, keeping the thread below point of needle. Secure loop by bringing thread over loop and going down at 2.
Fig. 7

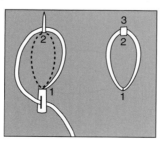

Running Stitch: Referring to Fig. 8, make a series of straight stitches with stitch length equal to the space between stitches.
Fig. 8

Satin Stitch: Referring to Fig. 9, come up at odd numbers and go down at even numbers with the stitches touching but not overlapping.
Fig. 9

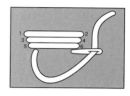

Stem Stitch: Referring to Fig. 10, come up at 1. Keeping the thread below the stitching line, go down at 2 and come up at 3. Go down at 4 and come up at 5.
Fig. 10

Straight Stitch: Referring to Fig. 11, come up at 1 and go down at 2.
Fig. 11

GENERAL INSTRUCTIONS (continued)
PLASTIC CANVAS

Gobelin Stitch: Referring to Fig. 1, work stitch over 2 or more threads or intersections. The number of threads or intersections may vary according to the chart.
Fig. 1

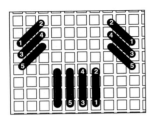

Backstitch: Refferring to Fig. 2, work stitch over completed stitches to outline or define. It is sometimes worked over more than one thread. Backtsitch may also be used to cover canvas.
Fig. 2

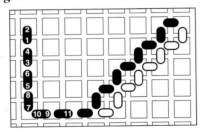

Cross Stitch: This stitch is composed of two stitches. The top of each cross must always be made in the same direction (Fig. 3).
Fig. 3

French Knot: Referring to Fig. 4, bring needle up through hole; wrap yarn once around needle and insert needle in same hole, holding end of yarn with non-stitching fingers. Tighten knot, then pull needle through canvas, holding yarn until it must be released.
Fig. 4

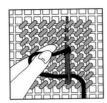

Overcast Stitch: This stitch covers the edge of the plastic canvas and joins pieces of canvas. It may be necessary to go through the same hole more than once to get even coverage on the edge, especially at the corners (Fig. 5).
Fig. 5

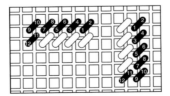

Tent Stitch: Referring to Fig. 6, work stitch in vertical or horizontal rows over one intersection.
Fig. 6

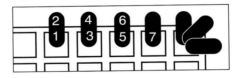

Mosiac Stitch: This three-stitch pattern forms small squares (Fig. 7).
Fig. 7

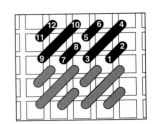

MULTI-LOOP BOWS

Making a multi-loop bow: For first streamer, measure desired length of streamer from one end of ribbon and twist ribbon between fingers.

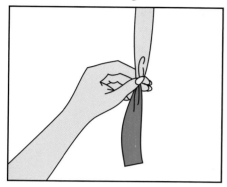

For first loop, keep right side of ribbon facing out and fold ribbon to front to form desired-size loop; gather between fingers.

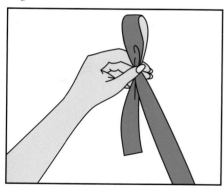

Fold ribbon to back to form another loop; gather between fingers. Continue to form loops, varying size as desired, until bow is desired size.

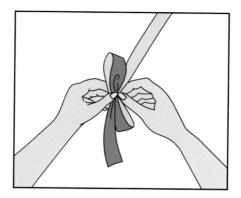

For remaining streamer, trim ribbon to desired length.

Follow project instructions to secure bow. If project instructions don't indicate a method for securing bow, wrap a length of wire around center of bow with ends at back. Hold wire ends with one hand and twist bow with the other hand to tighten wire. If desired, wrap a short length of ribbon around bow center and glue ends together at back, covering wire. Use wire ends to secure bow to project or trim ends close to bow and glue bow to project.

Arrange loops and trim ribbon ends as desired.

CUTTING A FABRIC CIRCLE

Matching right sides, fold fabric square in half from top to bottom and in half again from left to right.

Refer to project instructions for diameter of fabric circle; determine radius of circle by dividing diameter in half. Tie one end of string to fabric marking pencil. Insert thumbtack through string the determined radius from pencil. Insert thumbtack through fabric as shown in Fig. 1 and mark cutting line. Cut along drawn line through all fabric layers. Unfold circle.
Fig. 1

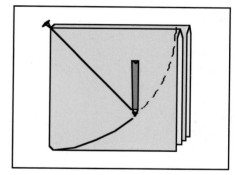

MAKING A POM-POM

Cut a 3" square of cardboard. Wind yarn around cardboard about 100 times. Carefully slip the yarn off the cardboard and firmly knot an 18" length of yarn around middle. Leave yarn ends long enough to attach pom-pom to project. Cut loops and trim to shape pom-pom into a smooth ball. Fluff pom-pom by rolling between hands. Use long yarn ends to attach pom-pom to project.

CREDITS

To Ann Townsend, who designed Plastic Canvas Gift Bags on page 112, and to Connie McGaughey, Judy Shirley, and Judy Simmons, who assisted in making and testing the projects in this book, we say thank you for your excellent work.

We especially want to recognize photographers David Hale, Mark Mathews, Larry Pennington, Karen Shirey, and Ken West of Peerless Photography, and Jerry R. Davis of Jerry Davis Photography, all of Little Rock, Arkansas, for their time, patience, and excellent work.

Leisure Arts would like to thank Husqvarna Viking Sewing Machine Company of Cleveland, Ohio, for providing the sewing machines used to make some of the projects in this book.